Praise for *One, Holy, Catholic, and Apostolic*

"This book by Cardinal Joseph Zen is an important witness of the love that His Eminence has for the 'one, holy, catholic, and apostolic' Church, and this explains also his warnings about the present crisis of the Church. In this regard, it is important to read carefully what he has to say, especially about the 'Synod on Synodality.' It is a valuable book to reflect on some important Catholic truths that today appear almost forgotten."

—+ Athanasius Schneider, Auxiliary Bishop of the Archdiocese of St. Mary in Astana

"Cardinal Joseph Zen is one of the great Christian witnesses of our time, a man full of faith who lives the joy of the gospel. His words of wisdom will, I hope, inspire Catholics around the world to believe as firmly as he does."

—George Weigel, Distinguished Senior Fellow and William E. Simon Chair in Catholic Studies, Ethics and Public Policy Center

"Cardinal Zen is a giant of the Faith."

—Paul Mariani, S.J., Edmund Campion, S.J. Professor, Department of History, Santa Clara University

"In this book, Cardinal Zen shows himself to be a wise and learned shepherd. Most of the chapters are taken from homilies, pastoral letters, and other pronouncements made during his time as the coadjutor and then bishop of Hong Kong (1996–2009). The cardinal touches on a wide range of topics, including moral theology, eschatology, sexuality, the priesthood, and marriage. In his final chapter, he offers his insights and concerns about the current Synod on Synodality. While recognizing synods as a historical reality, he examines competing views on what synodality actually means for the life of the Church today. This book should be of interest to all Catholics who share Cardinal Zen's passionate love for the one, holy, catholic, and apostolic Church. Even those who might disagree with some of his views will find his points provocative and engaging."

—Robert Fastiggi, Ph.D., Professor of Dogmatic Theology, Sacred Heart Major Seminary, Detroit

"A book by Cardinal Zen is earning the highest attention today. Cardinal Zen is a rock of orthodoxy in a time when the Church in Western countries is weakened by the loss of faith. Hearing the voice of this holy bishop is, in this era of heresy and ignorance, a comfort and gives hope that the Holy Spirit has not left the Church."

—Martin Mosebach, writer

"In this insightful book, sorely needed in a time such as ours in the Church, Joseph Cardinal Zen shows that the Church is at a crossroads on the reception of the ecclesiology of Vatican II in *Lumen Gentium*: the liberal/progressive and conservative/neo-traditionalist. Cardinal Zen addresses an issue of continuing urgency in post–Vatican II theology—namely, harmonious development of that ecclesiology, as in the writings of Popes Paul VI, John Paul II, and Benedict XVI, or deviation from, and rupture with, Catholic tradition. The author is to be applauded for his efforts to implement the authentic teachings of the council."

—Dr. Eduardo Echeverria, Professor of Philosophy and Theology, Sacred Heart Major Seminary, Detroit

"In each generation, often in moments of crisis, there emerge unique men and women endowed with a combination of clarity of mind and courage who speak out in so compelling a manner that their words can bring insight and encouragement when confusion, doubt, and discouragement prevail. One of those contemporary voices is that of His Eminence Joseph Cardinal Zen, a man whose humility may sometimes cloak his intelligence, strength, and insight. His fidelity to the apostolic tradition, which pervades these pages, will stir the soul and engender boldness in confidently speaking the truth."

—Fr. Robert Sirico, President Emeritus and Co-Founder, The Acton Institute

"This book by Cardinal Joseph Zen is a book needed in our time of great confusion in the Church. In his text, Cardinal Zen reminds everyone what the Church really is and what the Church always should be, a Church that Christ has given us for the salvation of humanity—not a sort of NGO. The words of the former bishop of Hong Kong are a wake-up call for all those who have forgotten what the Church is about and what should be her nature and structure. The pages on the Synod on Synodality also cause us to think about what is at stake in our day, and they should be considered with our utmost attention."

—Gerhard Cardinal Müller, Archbishop-bishop emeritus of Regensburg

One, Holy, Catholic, and Apostolic

Also by Cardinal Zen
from Sophia Institute Press:

Cardinal Zen's Advent Reflections

Cardinal Zen's Lenten Reflections

Cardinal Joseph Zen

One, Holy, Catholic, and Apostolic

From the Church of the Apostles to the "Synodal" Church

Edited by Aurelio Porfiri

SOPHIA INSTITUTE PRESS
Manchester, New Hampshire

Cover design by Updatefordesign Studio.

On the cover: vector of St. Peter's Basilica by Yoko Design / Shutterstock (158708765).

Interior image of Vatican seal by P-JR—this vector image includes elements that have been taken or adapted from this file: CC BY-SA 3.0, https://commons.wikimedia.org/w/index.php?curid=34002887.

Sophia Institute Press
Box 5284, Manchester, NH 03108
1-800-888-9344

www.SophiaInstitute.com

Sophia Institute Press® is a registered trademark of Sophia Institute.

paperback ISBN 979-8-88911-078-1
ebook ISBN 979-8-88911-079-8

Library of Congress Control Number: 2024938710

First printing

Contents

One, Holy, Catholic, and Apostolic

Introduction

by Aurelio Porfiri

"I believe in one, holy, catholic, and apostolic Church." This is what we say in the Creed, and this is what we are called to believe firmly as Catholics. This is the Church Jesus Christ entrusted to the apostles with Peter as their leader and to their successors.

During her two thousand years of history, the Church has passed through periods of great triumph but also of great suffering. How will the present moment be judged by historians? Probably as a period of great crisis. In fact, we are witnessing a crisis of faith: vocations have drastically diminished, and participation in the sacraments is ever poorer. It is noteworthy that this crisis shows a particular virulence precisely in Europe which had been Catholic for so many centuries. For this reason, today's crisis is the more remarkable, and everyone offers his or her own interpretation of what we are living through.

The Lord has always come to the aid of His Church in times of danger, and the most efficacious instrument has been the succession of Synods and Councils (the two terms are interchangeable) beginning with that in Jerusalem which became the model for all successive Councils. The Holy Spirit, promised by Jesus, guided the primitive Church in clarifying the great trinitarian mysteries as well as those of the divine-human nature of Jesus. The Council of Trent; with its untiring labor that lasted eighteen years (1545–1563) under three pontiffs, placed the foundation for a true reform of the Church *in capite et in membris* (also called the "Counter Reform"), which carried out a defense against the Protestant Reformation.

A recent Council, the Second Vatican Council, was certainly the most majestic in history. The central theme of this Council was the Church as the sacrament of our union with God and of unity among men. Finishing the work interrupted at the First Vatican Council, this one developed the concept of the collegiality of the bishops, the successors of the apostles, with and under the Roman Pontiff, the successor of Peter.

Sixty years have passed since the conclusion of that Ecumenical Council, and still we find ourselves in grave turmoil precisely regarding ecclesiology. Obviously, the Council should not be blamed for this. The fact is that, despite the clear pronouncements of *Lumen Gentium* and the subsequent faithful interpretation by Popes Paul VI, John Paul II, and Benedict XVI, adversarial forces have not been lacking on both the right and the left. On the right, ultraconservative traditionalists judge the Council to have been a rupture in the Church's tradition. On the left, ultraprogressives affirm that the so-called spirit of the Council has not fully developed its impetus for *aggiornamento* and so propose a radical revolution that opens wide the doors to the spirit of the world.

Cardinal Joseph Zen, born in Shanghai in 1932, was received by the Salesian Fathers as an adolescent. At sixteen, he was transferred to Hong Kong and entered the Salesians of Don Bosco (1948). He received his initial formation and worked for three years in the field of education in Salesian schools in Hong Kong (1948–1955). He was then sent to Turin, Italy (1955), to continue his studies at the Pontifical Salesian University and obtained degrees in philosophy (1957) and theology (1961). He was ordained a priest in 1961. In Rome, he obtained his doctorate in philosophy (1964).

These were the years of preparation for the Second Vatican Council, which was getting underway. Finding himself in the midst of that great "wind of Pentecost" (as some defined it) and living in an international environment rubbing shoulders with illustrious professors and intelligent companions at the Pontifical University was truly an extraordinary grace for Fr. Zen. This prepared him, upon his return to Hong Kong (1964), to teach philosophy and theology in the Salesian seminary as well as in the diocesan seminary for more than fifty years (including the seven years from 1989 to 1996, when he was allowed to teach in seminaries in mainland China as well).

The reflections on ecclesiology that you are about to read are mostly taken from his Sunday homilies, pastoral letters, and other pronouncements during the period in which he was coadjutor bishop (1996–2002) and then ordinary bishop of Hong Kong (2002–2009).

Even after his period of episcopal service in the diocese, aware of the grave duty of every bishop to be the custodian of the sound doctrine of faith, he has intervened in current issues in the Church, showing himself a faithful disciple of Pope Benedict XVI, who made him a cardinal in 2006. Cardinal Zen insists that the reflections in this collection do not presume to offer a systematic ecclesiology; for such an investigation, he recommends that readers consult the Dogmatic Constitution *Lumen Gentium* as well as the Letter of Pope Benedict XVI in 2007 "To the Church that is in the People's Republic of China," in which he treats the issue of ecclesiology in the Chinese situation (Cardinal Zen discusses this letter at length in his book *For the Love of My People I Will Not Keep Silent*).

We would like to thank Annie, Reno, Law Wang Tat, and Pauline for the translation.

The Church is built on the apostles

Jesus entrusted the continuation of His mission to the apostles

The Gospel of Matthew was written mainly for the Jewish people, and he emphasized that the prophets' prophecies were fully fulfilled in Jesus. Jesus began preaching in Galilee, where there were many foreigners, or Gentiles. Matthew quoted the prophet saying, "for those who sat in the region and shadow of death light has dawned," bringing joy to them (4:16).

"Repent, for the kingdom of heaven is at hand" (Matt. 3:2). This is good news and a calling. The gate of the kingdom of Heaven has opened, you must enter! Salvation is laid before you; accept it! People are free to respond; some reject the light and remain in darkness. "But to all who received him, who believed in his name, he gave power to become children of God" (John 1:12).

Within this fundamental calling, some are called more specifically: "Come, follow me!" Calling the apostles to follow him was Jesus' first action when He began to preach. It also represented one of His fundamental choices: He wanted some people to live with Him, listen to His words, and watch His actions so they could inherit His work and testify for Him after He ascended into Heaven.

The Son of God became incarnate, became man, bringing the history of man to its final stage. As the Mediator between Heaven and man, He mended the covenant between God and man. He accomplished the plan of God's creation and won God's grace for everyone in a miraculous way. Jesus finished His salvation plan and ascended to Heaven in glory. This was followed by the time of the Holy Spirit. Of course, the Holy Spirit has been in the world since the Creation of the world, but the Paschal Mystery of Christ gained the solemn coming of the Holy Spirit and His abundant charism.

Jesus called a group of apostles to follow Him when He started preaching. The Gospel says Jesus spent a night in prayer to God before He called them. Their names are clearly listed in the Gospels, and Simon Peter is always the first on the list. Obviously, he was the leader of the apostles. The apostles were a group of very ordinary people who were mainly fishermen. And there was Matthew, who was a tax collector. Among them, Judas Iscariot was chosen and was entrusted to take care of the finances. But in the end, he betrayed Jesus. Jesus patiently nurtured the twelve apostles. They all determined to follow Him except the traitor. Even when they were weak and confused at times, Jesus never abandoned them. After His Resurrection, Jesus called them His brothers and met them several times over forty days. Under the confirmation and guidance of the Holy Spirit, they spread the gospel to all nations and bravely bore witness to the death and Resurrection of the Lord.

God's plan is wonderful and unpredictable. He likes to choose His helpers among people to complete His work. He chooses whomever He likes.

Jesus built his Church upon the apostles, not on a book. The Gospel written by inspiration of the Holy Spirit should also be explained in the living Sacred Tradition. Sacred Tradition, the Creed, and the Magisterium are indispensable elements of the Church. If I say, "I want Christ only in the Gospel. I don't want the Sacred Tradition; I don't want the Creed; I don't want the Magisterium," I can't find Christ at all. It is He who wants us to find Him in Sacred Tradition through the Creed and the Magisterium. It is He who appointed some people to be His instruments of grace.

Jesus' intention in calling the apostles was to have them to continue the work He had begun. He was different from other masters. While other masters set up schools at a specific location and take in apprentices, Jesus wandered around looking for lost sheep. The apostles were also sent to preach, to heal, and to exorcize demons. This was a very dynamic mission.

They were to take nothing but a walking stick on the road. The walking stick was for their journey, and the apostles were "travelers."

This mention of a walking stick reminds us that on the night when the Israelites left Egypt, when they consumed the lamb, they had to eat with their loins girded, sandals on their feet, and staff in hand; they had to eat it "in haste" (Exod. 12:11). They had to be ready to go at any time. Similarly, anywhere could be a shelter for the apostles, but they were always ready to depart.

The staff (walking stick) also reminds us that the flock follows the shepherd without fear of danger, for "thy rod and thy staff, they comfort me" (Ps. 23:4). The apostles shepherded Jesus' flock on His behalf. The staff was used for walking or directing the flock, and the rod was used for self-defense and protection of the flock.

Jesus said, "Take nothing for your journey" (Luke 9:3). The Apostle Paul also said, "Every athlete exercises self-control in all things" (1 Cor. 9:25). Of course, if one puts on heavy armor, he simply cannot run very fast, and he is bound to lose a footrace. Look at our many packed boxes when we move, or our technical equipment when we venture out to preach—should we not be ashamed? If we need so many sophisticated tools to carry out our work with confidence, then we are no longer relying on God's words.

The prophet Amos was called by the Lord to be His spokesman in Bethel, where he denounced the sins of the people and the king and prophesied the demise of the Northern Kingdom. The priest of Bethel, Amaziah, told him to go away, and never again prophesy in Bethel. Amos replied, "I am no prophet, nor a prophet's son; but I am a herdsman, and a dresser of sycamore trees" (Amos 7:14). He had no choice, as it was God who asked him to say those words. It was not a political plan plotted by him against the king. He was simply reciting the words of the Lord. Amos was not bound by any material benefits, and thus he was not afraid of speaking frankly.

Jesus left behind His words

When we count according to the number of years of the world's history, we can say Jesus "comes and goes in haste." The wonderful plan of God does not let generations of people see the face of Jesus. The Acts of the Apostles describes the Ascension of the Lord: "When he had said this, as they were looking on, he was lifted up, and a cloud took him out of their sight" (1:9).

What Jesus left behind was His "word," and it was also the "word" of the Father, "If a man loves me, he will keep my word, and my Father will love him" (John 14:23). Earlier Jesus said, "He who has my commandments and keeps them, he it is who loves me; and he who loves me will be loved by my Father, and I will love him and manifest myself to him" (John 14:21). That is to say, we still have another way to see Him, although we cannot see Him through our physical eyes.

People in the modern world prefer to "see" and wish to see everything. (Televisions have generally replaced radios.) Yet God wants us to "listen" more and to remember and obey what we hear.

The "word" is the great grace God has given us, and it is a grace among graces that the "Word" became incarnate, became man. Through God's "Word," the "Word" of truth, Jesus became our way, which leads us to life.

The Bible seems to have placed less emphasis on "seeing" than on "hearing:" "Blessed are those who have not seen and yet believe" (John 20:29). Our eyes see only the surface, while words can discuss the truth in depth. Sometimes our religion is also called the religion of the "book" (not a book of pictures, but a book of words). A man must read books (not only newspapers and magazines) if he wants to be mature.

Jesus left his "words" to His apostles and the Holy Spirit: "These things I have spoken to you, while I am still with you. But the Counselor, the Holy Spirit, whom the Father will send in my name, he will teach you all things, and bring to your remembrance all that I have said to you" (John 14:25–26).

Paragraph 65 of the *Catechism of the Catholic Church* (CCC) says, "Christ, the Son of God made man, is the Father's one, perfect and unsurpassable Word. In him he has said everything; there will be no other word than this one." Paragraph 66 says, "Yet even if Revelation is already complete, it has not been made completely explicit." Therefore, after His Ascension, Jesus and the Father solemnly sent forth the Holy Spirit to lead the apostles and the Church, generation after generation, to know all truth.

The members of the First Council of Jerusalem, apostles and presbyters, sent their representatives to Antioch to deliver the conclusion of the Council: "For it has seemed good to the Holy Spirit and to us …" (Acts 15:28). The Holy Spirit and the leadership of the Church have made many decisions throughout the history. The leaders of the Church are human; the Holy Spirit would not allow them to bring the Church down. Nor would the Holy Spirit miraculously impose on the Church a perfect, ready-made history. Instead, He patiently accompanies the Church to construct her history. If we look back objectively at the two thousand years of history, it is not difficult to appreciate the miraculous work of the Holy Spirit. He has protected the Church, which is like a small boat in a big ocean.

Some people disagree with the Church's using Greek cultural concepts to express the mystery of the Holy Trinity. But is it not invaluable to have a clear language system to ensure the unity and communication of faith?

Some people regard the Council of Trent, the encyclical *Quanta Cura* of Pope Pius IX, and the condemnation of modernism by Pope Pius X as refusing to keep up with the times. But when the germs invade a body, what the body needs urgently is medicine to prevent the spread of the virus. Medicines are not food, let alone delicacies. Some people do not accept the *Veritatis Splendor* of John Paul II, but in the face of rampant ethical relativism, how could the pope not speak out to defend objective moral value?

We certainly cannot replace our meals with medicines, which also carry side effects. Yet the Holy Spirit leads the Church to find medicine in the Bible and in Holy Tradition to resist fallacies and provides rich nutrition for the faithful. It is just that some people have problems with their appetite. Jesus said, "I thank thee, Father, Lord of heaven and earth, that thou hast hidden these things from the wise and understanding and revealed them to babes" (Matt. 11:25).

A Church of tradition

Where do we find the word of God? "In many and various ways God spoke of old to our fathers by the prophets; but in these last days he has spoken to us by a Son" (Heb. 1:1–2). God has spoken to living people and has asked some to write down these precious words. The Church firmly believes that, in addition to the Bible, God entrusts His Word to living people as well.

Jesus passed His words on to the apostles, "Go into all the world and preach the gospel to the whole creation" (Mark 16:15). "Go therefore and make disciples of all nations, baptizing them in the name of the Father and of the Son and of the Holy Spirit, teaching them to observe all that I have commanded you" (Matt. 28:19–20). In order to enable the apostles to undertake this monumental task, before His Ascension, Jesus Christ promised to be with them "always, to the close of the age" (Matt. 28:20). He also promised to send the Spirit of truth, who would then guide the apostles to understand "all truth" (John 16:13).

This dynamic transmission accomplished in the Holy Spirit is called "Divine Tradition." This "holy heritage of faith," contained in Sacred Scripture and Tradition, is what St. Paul calls "the sacred deposit of faith" in 1 Timothy 6:20. The apostles entrusted this "sacred deposit of faith" to the whole of the Church (CCC 84), but "the task of giving an authentic interpretation of the Word of God, whether in its written form or in the form of Tradition, has been entrusted to the living teaching office of the Church alone" (CCC 85). "At the divine command and with the help of the Holy Spirit, it [the living teaching office] listens to this devotedly, guards it with dedication and expounds it faithfully" (CCC 86).

Of course, safekeeping the "sacred deposit of faith" is nothing like keeping pearls in a jewelry box and passing them on exactly as they are. This sacred heritage is alive and dynamic. Just as life does, it possesses two inseparable characteristics: "continuity" and "breakthrough." The Word of God never changes, but it develops its vitality in every new situation from generation to generation.

In order to faithfully preserve and proclaim the Word of God, the apostles felt that it was "not right that we should give up preaching the word of God to serve tables," so they suggested appointing deacons so that they could devote themselves "to prayer and to the ministry of the word" (Acts 6:2, 4).

The Church documents in the modern era all emphasize that a priest's primary function is to serve the Word of God, followed by the administration of the sacraments and the leadership of the community.[1] I believe that, from the perspective of most believers, their greatest expectation from their priests is to hear the Word of God from them. Priests need not be eloquent, but they should meditate on the Word in the Holy Spirit, experience it in life, and express it from the bottom of their heart.

One major benefit to celibacy is that it allows the priests to express their "zeal about the things of the Lord" and serve the Word of the Lord without distraction (1 Cor. 7:32–35).

Change, unchanged?

"Jesus Christ, the everlasting One." "Everlasting One" certainly means eternity without any changes, so we immediately have a question: Is it better to change or be unchanged? If things don't change, won't they be stale and dull? Isn't the

[1] See Pope John Paul II, apostolic exhortation *Pastores Dabo Vobis* (March 25, 1992), no. 26.

beauty of this world in its variety, which is new every day? Perhaps we can agree with this saying: that when we are satisfied, we do not want to change, and when we are not satisfied, we want to change. In fact, change is not necessarily an improvement, and improvement is not necessarily sustainable. It is said that there is no eternal banquet in the world. We have to admit that what we are seeking is never-ending happiness, which is absolutely not old-fashioned, as the human heart is like that.

The Letter to the Hebrews says, "Remember your leaders, those who spoke to you the word of God" (13:7). St. Augustine in his youth had gone many wrong ways, and finally, he said, "O Lord, our hearts are restless until they rest in You."[2]

Christ, the everlasting One

Jesus invites us by saying, "Come and see" (John 1:39). "You see who I really am?" Peter saw clearly by the inspiration of the Holy Spirit: "You are the Christ!" (Matt. 16:16). Let the Holy Spirit also help us to see clearly that Christ is our only Savior; He is the everlasting one in the ever-changing world.

[2] St. Augustine, *Confessions* 1, 1.

The Church is built on the apostles

The unchangeable precedes change, eternity creates time, and human history is an extension of the love of the Holy Trinity.

The Father begets the Son, and the Father and the Son love each other in the Holy Spirit. This is a constant, eternal, and ever-new mystery.

The unchanged participates in change

The Father created us in Christ and made our destiny adoption to Himself through Jesus Christ. The Father sent the Spirit of the Son to cry out in our hearts, "Abba, Father!" From now on, the unchanged participates in change, the Word dwells in us, and from His fullness, we have all received, grace in place of grace already given (John 1:16).

This grace is called salvation because in history we have brought about an unfortunate big change: sin. But Christ reversed that unfortunate situation and accomplished the greatest change in history: the Paschal Mystery, cleansing us through His blood, conquering sin, and conquering death.

Christ has triumphed; salvation has been accomplished

Let us declare to all people, "Brothers and friends, be aware: God's salvation is upon you, Jesus Christ has dwelled in your hearts. Entrust your burdens, worries, and pain to Him!"

I'm afraid someone will answer us and say, "We don't know your God and will not believe in your Jesus."

"This is a big misunderstanding. Our God is also your God, and our Jesus is also your Savior. You don't know Him yet, but He knows you, and He loves you. How the salvation of Jesus came to you I do not know, but I don't need to know; what I know for sure is that Jesus has crazily fallen in love with you with all His heart, has dedicated Himself to you, and will not give up on you."

Lift up your voice to proclaim the good news

Preaching is not to say to others, "You should be quick to join our religion; otherwise, you will not be saved." Preaching is actually "to be sent to proclaim the Savior, who is already here." God "desires all men to be saved and to come to the knowledge of the truth" (1 Tim. 2:4). "Being sent to preach" doesn't make us proud, and "to declare that Jesus is the only Savior" is never self-righteousness. We know that salvation is not something we deserve. The Bible says, "Blessed is he whose transgression is forgiven, whose sin is covered. Blessed is the man to whom the Lord imputes no iniquity" (Ps. 32:1–2). We have received this blessing, so how can we not lift up our voices and proclaim this good news to the ends of the earth? "Woe to me if I do not preach the gospel!" (1 Cor. 9:16).

St. Thérèse of Lisieux, the patron saint of missions and Doctor of the Church

Pope John Paul II declared St. Thérèse of Lisieux patron saint of missions and a Doctor of the Church—an outstanding teacher of the Church. Yet she did not travel far to preach, nor did she write sophisticated texts. But from her monastery, she spoke the essence of the gospel to mankind: "God is love, the love that never changes. Let us trust in His love and live in him by love."

In life that is ever-changing, this is the eternal truth. The mission of preaching is to introduce to people the God who is everlasting and loves them forever. He loves each of us unconditionally, freely, and without regret.

May the Holy Spirit of Christ lead us, like St. Thérèse of Lisieux, to proclaim, practice, and become love in the Church.

Whether tomorrow will be better, from a human perspective, we do not know. But we must move forward with confidence. The foundation of our confidence is Jesus Christ, who "is the same yesterday and today and forever" (Heb. 13:8).

Discernment in the Holy Spirit

Let us first look at the mission of the Holy Spirit in the Church, and then talk about how to discern His direction and fruits. The Second Vatican Council's Dogmatic Constitution on the Church, *Lumen Gentium*, is undoubtedly our best guide.

A. The Works of the Holy Spirit in the Church

Paragraph 4 of *Lumen Gentium* says that the Holy Spirit "bears witness to the fact that [we] are adopted sons." I believe this is the most crucial task of the Holy Spirit. From eternity, the Father, through the Holy Spirit, called His Son "my beloved Son"; from eternity, through the Holy Spirit, the Son called His Father "Abba, Father!" Through the Holy Spirit, whom Jesus earned for us by His suffering, we, together with Him, cry out to the Father, "Abba, Father!" This is the Holy Spirit who affirms and guarantees our identities as adopted sons.

Paragraph 4 of *Lumen Gentium* also points out two crucial tasks of the Holy Spirit: to guide the Church in the "way of all truth" and to unify the Church "in communion and in works of ministry."

In addition, paragraphs 4, 7, and 12, *Lumen Gentium* says that the Holy Spirit "gives His different gifts for the welfare of the Church" (Eph. 4:11–12; 1 Cor. 12:8–11) and "adorns [the Church] with His fruits" (Gal. 5:22).

B. How to discern the movement of the Holy Spirit

How to discern the movement of the Holy Spirit? The basic answer is to be found in the same constitution, where the Holy Spirit has placed an "insurance institution" within the Church. Paragraph 4 of *Lumen Gentium* says, "The Holy Spirit both equips and directs with hierarchical and charismatic gifts."

Paragraph 7 says, "What has a special place among these gifts is the grace of the apostles to whose authority the Spirit Himself subjected even those who were endowed with charisms."

Section 12 says more obviously, "Extraordinary gifts are not to be sought after, nor are the fruits of apostolic labor to be presumptuously expected from their use; but judgment as to their genuinity and proper use belongs to those who are appointed leaders in the Church."

Of course, St. Paul the Apostle also reminds us in 1 Thessalonians 5:19–22 of how those who manage the Church should fulfill this responsibility. He said, "Do not quench the Spirit, do not despise prophesying, but test everything; hold fast what is good, abstain from every form of evil."

Do not think that this is an easy task. This responsibility is so heavy that even St. Paul asked the faithful to sympathize with their leaders (see 1 Thess. 5:12–13; Heb. 13:17).

Irresponsible shepherds are called in the Bible "dumb dogs [that] cannot bark" (Isa. 56:10).

C. A few examples

Let us try to apply this criterion to a few concrete examples:

1. On seeking the truth
2. On the discernment of charisms

1. *Seeking the truth.* All the People of God have the role of prophets. If, together with the bishops, under the leadership of the Magisterium, they agree with the doctrine or the ethics handed down by the apostles, they cannot be wrong. But the individual faithful, priests, and even bishops are not morally infallible. If bishops and priests, in particular, use their status and position to criticize the teachings of the Church openly, it is obviously unfair, as their clerical status is imparted by magisterial authority.

Pope John Paul II said, "Theological opinions constitute neither the rule nor the norm of our teaching. Its authority is derived, by the assistance of the Holy Spirit and in communion *cum Petro et sub Petro*, from our fidelity to the Catholic faith which comes from the Apostles."[3]

[3] Pope John Paul II, encyclical *Veritatis Splendor* (*The Splendor of Truth*) (August 6, 1993), no. 116.

2. *Discerning charisms*. On the evening of May 30, 1998, about five hundred thousand members of different charismatic groups and ecclesial movements within the Church packed into St. Peter's Square. Pope John Paul II invited them to celebrate the eve of Pentecost. The pope greatly appreciated the rise and development of these movements. He said that it was one of the fruits of Vatican II, and these movements have brought a new impetus to the Church, but he also said frankly that the movement "is sometimes even disruptive. This has given rise to questions, uneasiness, and tensions; at times it has led to presumptions and excesses on the one hand, and on the other, to numerous prejudices and reservations." "At times, the movement also brought shocks, and even inevitably caused doubts and unease, thus creating tension." He added that sometimes, in these movements, there is overconfidence and a lack of moderation as well as some prejudices and reservations in the face of these movements. "It was a testing period for their fidelity, an important occasion for verifying the authenticity of their charisms. Today a new stage is unfolding before you: that of ecclesial maturity."[4]

[4] See Pope John Paul II, speech during a meeting with ecclesial movements and new communities (May 30, 1998), no. 6.

The pope asked, "How is it possible to safeguard and guarantee a charism's authenticity?" The answer is: "It is essential in this regard that every movement submit to the discernment of the competent ecclesiastical authority.... May this element of trusting obedience to the Bishops, the successors of the Apostles, in communion with the Successor of Peter never be lacking in the Christian formation provided by your movements!"[5]

Charismatic reform?

Charisms are bestowed by the Holy Spirit, and it is the responsibility of the Church to discern and direct their use. Charisms may also have the mission of reforming the Church and the hierarchy, such as in St. Francis of Assisi, whose mission was to influence his contemporary Church leaders and return to the spirit of poverty in accordance with the gospel. He submitted the plan for the establishment of his religious order to the Holy See for approval. The Holy Spirit helped him especially and made the pope see in a dream a monk who looked like a beggar holding up in his hands the crumbling Basilica of St. John Lateran, the cathedral of the pope. Historically, many popes and

[5] Ibid., no. 8.

bishops made saints suffer, but the saints did not doubt the authority of those popes and bishops. Here we can see the difference between saints and ordinary people. Some people think that they have a mission to fight against Church authorities in order to display their charisms. How much harm do such people do to themselves and to the People of God in the end? This behavior can be seen from time to time in history.

Is the Church conservative and undemocratic?

Conservative progressive are provocative adjectives without accurate content. Was Pope John XXIII conservative or progressive? He recited three Rosaries a day, but it was he who called the revolutionary Ecumenical Council. Originally, the Church has always been conservative, and her mission is to protect and safeguard the treasures of Tradition. Protecting Tradition is not sealing a dead thing but refers to the continuation of faith in life. In modern times, popes are both conservative and progressive leaders.

As for democracy, although the Church does not have a democratic system, the Church in modern times quite complies with the spirit of democracy when handling business. Obvious examples are the process of compiling the Catholic

Catechism and holding bishops' representative conferences. Before making any important decisions, the popes consult extensively.

D. The fruit of the Holy Spirit

There is another way to discern: a good or bad tree is determined by its fruit. In the Letter to the Galatians and elsewhere, St. Paul lists some of the fruits of the Holy Spirit: "love, joy, peace, patience, kindness, goodness, faithfulness, gentleness, self-control" (5:22–23). Some people make a good point: there is only one fruit, and that is love. But if everyone may say their actions are out of love, how can we discern true from false, right from wrong? Again, a longer list could help. We could add to the list humility, docility, and caring about unity within the Church.

It is never easy to discern charisms. "The wind blows where it wills, and you hear the sound of it, but you do not know whence it comes or whither it goes" (John 3:8). One may ask: What kind of wind is it? Elijah met God in the breeze, but on the day of Pentecost when the Holy Spirit came, there was a storm instead (see 1 Kings 19:9–13; Acts 2:2). No matter how the Holy Spirit wants to blow, we must let go of our small egos and open our hearts to follow His movement!

The salt of the earth

Jesus also said, "You are the salt of the earth; but if salt has lost its taste, how shall its saltness be restored?" (Matt. 5:13). Salt is a very common thing that is not worth much money. But I have heard of people smuggling salt at the risk of their lives in war. Food without salt is not tasty to eat. Lack of salt in the body may also cause many diseases.

I remember that I baptized babies in the church every Sunday while studying in Rome.[6] The most interesting part in the old ritual for Baptism was putting salt (which symbolizes wisdom) in the babies' mouths. The babies' reactions varied. Some ate with relish while some cried aloud when they tasted it. Actually, we are not proposing to eat salt in that way; it should be mixed with food to make the food taste good.

God seems to have long known that the world will be "secularized" eventually. The faithful will be a minority. Many people are only busy earning their bread and butter. Money is the only thing they care about. If the faithful also live as if God does not exist, the world will be like tasteless food. The faithful in this secularized world act as salt when

[6] The cardinal studied for his doctorate in philosophy in Rome between 1961 and 1964.–Ed.

they remind people of the end of life. The problem of earning our bread and butter still needs to be resolved, but it is not the only dimension in our lives.

Utilitarianism and pragmatism pervade society. People are becoming more and more unfamiliar with "meaning" and "ideal" and even regard them as dangerous, poisonous things. "Don't talk about absolute principles and eternal truth. Dogmatism is no good. Let us resolve practical problems in a down-to-earth way. Business is business; politics is politics. Don't talk too much about conscience." People laugh at the poor but not at prostitutes. Those who do not know how to wheel and deal or take advantage of others are fools.

But, in this way, do people really solve their problems? On the contrary, these "truths" have created countless problems for mankind, causing immeasurable suffering. Man becomes cruel and evil.

Christians are the salt of the earth; the truth of the Beatitudes is to be the salt of the earth. I hope that through our testimony of love, modern people who have lost their direction can find the meaning of life.

Peter the rock, the first among the apostles

Peter, the rock and the shepherd

Peter is the leader of the apostles. The Gospel gives a very detailed description of him. After working hard all night and having caught nothing, he and his partners filled their boats with fish because of the words Jesus spoke to them. Witnessing this miracle, Peter fell to his knees before Jesus and asked Jesus to depart from him, acknowledging that he was not worthy of friendship with the Lord. But Jesus told him, "Henceforth you will be catching men" (Luke 5:10).

Peter was an impulsive person. When he saw Jesus walking on the sea, he wanted to try too. Jesus said, "Come." Peter got out of the boat and began to walk on the water. But he became frightened when he saw how strong the wind was (Matt. 14:28–30). On the mountain where Jesus was transfigured, Peter was very excited. He promised to make a tent each for Jesus, Moses, and Elijah. Indeed, the Gospel says that he did not know what he was saying (Matt. 17:4; Luke 9:33).

God enabled Peter to recognize the identity of Jesus and confess that He is the Messiah. Jesus changed Simon's name to Peter (the rock) and said that He would build His Church upon this rock (Matt. 16:16–19). But soon after, Jesus severely rebuked Peter because he judged from a human perception and opposed the idea that Jesus should suffer (Matt. 16:22–23). (Purely from a human point of view, Peter did have a generous heart and sincerely loved his teacher.)

Later, Jesus asked Peter to go fishing and to take the coin from the mouth of the first fish he caught. "When you open its mouth you will find a shekel; take that and give it to them [for a tax] for me and for yourself" (Matt. 17:24–27). How meaningful it is: "Me and you" have become one, sharing the same fate.

Jesus said His soul was sorrowful even to death when He prayed in Gethsemane (see Matt. 26:38). He was then caught and tried, but He never resisted. Peter witnessed all this, and his faith was shaken. He once swore that he would not be afraid even if he had to die with Jesus. But Peter dared not say he was a disciple of Jesus before the guards and the maid. Just as he was saying this, the cock crowed, and the Lord turned and looked at Peter; and Peter remembered the word of the Lord, how He had said to him, "This very night, before the cock crows, you will deny me three times." He went out and began to weep bitterly (Matt. 26:34, 75). After that, Peter was not overconfident anymore. After His resurrection, Jesus asked Peter three times, "Do you love me?" Peter humbly said to Jesus, "Lord, you know everything; you know that I love you." Jesus still entrusted His sheep to his care (John 21:15–17).

Jesus chose this disciple for the foundation of His Church, and accepted, reformed, and strengthened him. Almighty God had decided to use a weak man for His work.

The wonderful gift of having a leader in the Church

For us faithful today, it is much easier to appreciate God's profound wisdom! The relevance of the pope's primacy becomes more and more apparent through the continuous self-understanding of the Church in history by the light of the Holy Spirit. More and more we can see what a precious gift this is and how well it fits into a world that has become a "global village." All mankind is one Church, one sheepfold with one shepherd, one leader—the successor of Peter, the Roman Pontiff.

When I was young, in the Shanghai Diocese, we always had to sing "Oremus pro Pontifice" during the Benediction of the Blessed Sacrament. "Let us pray for our Pope, that the Lord may preserve him, give him life, make him blessed upon the earth, and hand not his soul over to his enemies." The leading voice sang, "*Tu es Petrus*" (You are Peter [the rock]), and the faithful replied enthusiastically, "*Et super hanc petram aedificabo Ecclesiam meam*" (Upon this rock I will build my Church). As a young boy, I was so proud to be able to sing that long sentence in perfect Latin!

In these seventy-five years of ups and downs for the Church of our motherland, "Peter's rock" has become the touchstone of her faith, and papal primacy has become the mark of the test. How many faithful laid down their lives for this truth and died in prisons and labor camps? Many brothers and sisters offered their most precious twenty or thirty years of life behind bars. They peacefully and joyfully declared to all mankind that the invisible and intangible God was the Creator and Lord of the world.

Over the years, the antiphon to pray for the pope has seldom been heard. There was a time when it was forbidden to mention the pope. How the faithful rejoiced later when it was possible to pray for the pope again during Mass! The hearts of the Chinese faithful, whether of the open or underground church communities, have never left the pope. During the 1999 Synod of Bishops, I could confirm this to my brother bishops. Unfortunately I cannot say the same thing today: there are now really two different churches.

The Shepherd and the Lamb

Jesus is the Good Shepherd because the flock belongs to Him. The Creation and salvation have made us all His flock, and especially the work of redemption has demanded of Him an enormous price.

The Exodus recounts that the Israelites were saved by the blood of the lamb. Jesus was the Lamb "slaughtered by being hanged on the cross" (see Acts 5:27–32, 40–41); Deuteronomy says, "a hanged man is accursed by God" (21:23). Jesus was innocent but for our sake, God "made Him to be sin" (2 Cor. 5:21).

But Acts of the Apostles repeats, "God exalted him at his right hand" (5:31; cf. 2:33). Chapter 5 of Revelation says the Lamb was praised twice:

1. Countless angels cried out loud, "Worthy is the Lamb who was slain, to receive power and wealth and wisdom and might and honor and glory and blessing" (v. 12).

2. "Every creature in heaven and on earth and under the earth and in the sea, and all therein, [said], 'To him who sits upon the throne and to the Lamb be blessing and honor and glory and might for ever and ever!' " (v. 13)

The Acts of the Apostles says, "God exalted him … as Leader and Savior" (5:31).

The Lamb was willing to be slaughtered. Through His sacrifice, He gained the status of a king and has assumed the role of a Good Shepherd. The Priest turned into the sacrifice, and the Lamb became the Shepherd.

"Good Shepherd the First" passed His mission to "Good Shepherd the Second." "Simon, son of John, do you love me more than these?" (John 21:15). "Love" is the only question in the examination. Peter appeared less confident than before the Passion of Jesus, and he answered, "Yes, Lord, you know that I love you" (John 21:15). Jesus asked him thrice, allowing him to make up for the three times when he denied his Master. Jesus accepted his three declarations and entrusted him with His flock, naming him "Good Shepherd the Second," and predicted that he would die for Him. As Good Shepherd the First shepherds His flock, Good Shepherd the Second did the same: he laid down his life for the sheep.

"When you are old, you will stretch out your hands, and another will gird you and carry you where you do not wish to go" (John 21:17). This description naturally brings us back to the prophecy of Isaiah: "He was oppressed, and he was afflicted, yet he opened not his mouth; like a lamb that is led to the slaughter, and like a sheep that before its shearers is dumb, so he opened not his mouth" (53:7).

The Acts of the Apostles describes how the prophecy of Jesus was gradually fulfilled in Peter. Peter told the high priest: "We must obey God rather than men." Thus, the council "beat them … and let them go. Then they left the presence of the council, rejoicing that they were counted worthy to suffer dishonor for the name" (5:29, 40–41).

The apostles and the Church community kept bearing witness to the Resurrection of Christ: they testified with joy, charity, and poverty; and they also solemnly professed Jesus before the judges. Many of them shared the glory of martyrdom.

When Peter endured insult for the name of Jesus, he was fulfilling his utmost pastoral responsibility. Obedience to God is the primary dimension of serving the faithful, and loyalty to God is also the most needed witness for the faithful in modern times.

In God's plan, the "shepherd" and the "lamb" have miraculously become inseparable roles. It would be a serious misunderstanding if we were reluctant to give ourselves up, putting ourselves in the center or treating God's sheep as if they were our sheep.

True leadership

Chapter 5 of the book of Isaiah is a "love song." A friend's loving care for his vineyard represents God's kindness to the house of Israel (His beloved seedlings). But His spouse was unfaithful and broke His heart: "What more was there to do for my vineyard, that I have not done in it?" (v. 4). Grieved by betrayed love, He gave up. Abandoned and trampled vineyards turned into wastelands. What a sad sight!

How touching is the lamentation sung while the faithful venerate the cross on Good Friday, "Alas, My people! Have I wronged you? What have I done to you? Please answer me! I have fought Egypt and their first born for you, but you scourged me and handed me over to the pagans." A sequence of "I have ... but you ..." describes our ingratitude.

A tragic scene described in the Gospel is that of the landlord of a vineyard who sends his servants to obtain the produce from his tenants, and the tenants kill the servants.

Finally, the landlord sends his son, and the tenants throw him out of the vineyard and kill him. The landlord finally "put those wretches to a miserable death" (Matt. 21:41).

The "love song" in chapter 5 of the book of Isaiah is a complaint against the house of Israel; the Gospel's parable of the tenants is aimed at the leadership of the people who seized and owned the vineyard that did not belong to them. Jesus directly pointed to the chief priests and Pharisees then; however, it is a warning for all group leaders.

In God's plan, all leaders are His tenants, and He entrusts them to manage His beloved vineyard. They cannot take it for themselves. Social and political leaders need to reflect, and religious leaders must also be vigilant.

In the *Catechism of the Catholic Church*, paragraph 1897 says, "Human society can be neither well-ordered nor prosperous unless it has some people invested with legitimate authority to preserve its institutions and to devote themselves as far as is necessary to work and care for the good of all."[7] Paragraph 1898 says, "Every human community needs an authority to govern it."[8] Paragraph 1899 says, "The authority required by the moral order derives from God:

[7] Quoting John XXIII, *Pacem in Terris* 46.

[8] Cf. Leo XIII, *Immortale Dei; Diuturnum illud.*

'Let every person be subject to the governing authorities' (Rom. 13:1–2; cf. 1 Pet. 2:13–17)." But paragraph 1902 adds, "Authority does not derive its moral legitimacy from itself. It must not behave in a despotic manner but must act for the common good."

It is unfortunate that what officials pursue too many times is not public welfare but self-interest. To get promoted and become rich, many put their conscience aside. Religious leaders can also be tempted by self-interest, and Judas is a representative figure. The history of the Church is full of such experiences, and it is especially tragic for a religious leader to commit such a crime. The Old Testament describes them as shepherds who know only how to consume milk, wear wool, and slaughter fatlings instead of pasturing their flock (see Ezek. 34:3).

The vineyards that failed the landlord's love, and the tenants who failed the landlord's trust, were severely punished. The Bible seems to describe an act of revenge—love turned into hatred. Of course, we know that God does not hate what He has created and that punishment is a natural effect of sin. Using the words *revenge* and *hatred* to describe God's response, however, can make us experience the heinousness of sin. Even in society and the Church, men will be particularly contemptuous of such behavior in a leader. The terrible effects of these evils can deter us; positive motives, however, are certainly more effective in sustaining our duty.

In Philippians 4:8, the Apostle Paul says, "Brethren, whatever is true, whatever is honorable, whatever is just, whatever is pure, whatever is lovely, whatever is gracious ... think about these things." Nobel ideals ensure our faithful service to God and to our brothers. It is a pity that society is full of "pragmatic" educational objectives, which can only cultivate a group of shrewd "interest calculators." This is definitely not what God expects from us.

In the Bible, God and Jesus apparently stand on the side of the people and are harsh toward leaders. Whether it is God in the book of Malachi facing the priests of the time (1:14; 2:1–2, 8–10) or Jesus confronting the scribes and the Pharisees (Matt. 23:1–12), they are strict. For today's priests, bishops, government officials, and leaders of any groups, these readings are a good opportunity for them to reflect.

Leaders are God's representatives. Their task is to be a bridge between Heaven and man. If they become obstacles instead of serving as bridges or passages between Heaven and man, they violate the will of God.

1. *Benefits.* Being a group leader is not a career but a calling. The appointees should not be too calculating about their interests but should care about pleasing God and serving the people. In chapter 1 of the book of Malachi, the Lord rebuked the priests for offering blind, lame, and sick animals as sacrifices. In chapter 23 of the Gospel of Matthew, Jesus said that the scribes and Pharisees devoured widows' property.

On the contrary, Paul the Apostle was always honest and hardworking. He never looked for occasions for material gains. While preaching the gospel, he worked day and night so as not to burden his fellow believers. The evangelizer had the right to be supported by the faithful, but Paul voluntarily renounced this right. He entrusted to them not only the gospel of God but also his life.

2. *Honor.* The pursuit of interests is the pursuit of worldly matters, while the quest for glory is to put oneself in the position of God. Leaders who engage in a cult of personality simply usurp the authority of God, which God does not approve of: "He has put down the mighty from their thrones, and exalted those of low degree" (Luke 1:52).

In the Gospel, Jesus rebuked the scribes and the Pharisees because they loved places of honor at banquets, seats of honor in synagogues, and greetings in marketplaces (see Matt. 23:6–7).

St. Paul could say to the Thessalonians, “Nor did we seek glory from men, whether from you or from others, though we might have made demands as apostles of Christ. But we were gentle among you, like a nurse taking care of her children” (1 Thess. 2:6–7).

3. *Truth.* To be a leader is to be God’s prophet and His spokesperson. A prophet should speak the Words of God instead of his own. A leader is a servant of God’s words, not a master. The master expects faithfulness from his servant.

In the book of Malachi, God told the priests, “For the lips of a priest should guard knowledge, and men should seek instruction from his mouth.... But you have turned aside from the way; you have caused many to stumble by your instruction.... You have not kept my ways but have shown partiality in your instruction” (2:7–9).

St. Paul could say, “Our appeal does not spring from error or uncleanness, nor is it made with guile; but just as we have been approved by God to be entrusted with the gospel, so we speak, not to please men, but to please God who tests our hearts. For we never used ... words of flattery” (1 Thess. 2:3–5).

By the positive and negative teaching materials in the Bible, we make three points of reflection. These three points are not independent of each other. The pursuit of interests and glory are pursuits of ourselves, telling the faithful to stay with us instead of leading them to God.

Not telling the truth, not daring to tell the truth, and not being willing to tell the truth because it may result in losing benefits or because it is not popular to go against the tide, we might use flattery to help us stay in power in society.

Fortunately, many honest, hardworking, humble, and kind shepherds are still among us. They work humbly and pass on Christ's gospel to the People of God via their words and deeds. May the Lord be glorified in them!

James and John, the sons of Zebedee, said to Jesus, "Grant us to sit, one at your right hand and one at your left, in your glory" (Mark 10:37). The Gospel of Matthew stated that it was their mother who came to Jesus and asked of Him, "Command that these two sons of mine may sit, one at your right hand and one at your left, in your kingdom" (20:21).

Whether in the Gospel of Mark or of Matthew, the request of the two brothers was after the third prediction of the Passion and Resurrection of Jesus, and before Jesus cured the blind men in Jericho. Did "in your glory" and "in your kingdom" refer to things after the Resurrection of Jesus? It seemed not. Those two brothers were like the blind men, completely oblivious to the prospect that Jesus pointed out. All they cared about was the glory of this world, the kingdom of this world.

The other apostles were no better than these two brothers. The Gospel mentions that "when the ten heard it, they began to be indignant at James and John" (Mark 10:41). Was it because they were asking Jesus for something inappropriate? It seems not! Each and every one of them wanted to sit on the right or the left of the throne of Jesus!

The dullness of the apostles should have disappointed Jesus, but He patiently continued to teach them, thus leaving us with this valuable lesson, "Whoever would be great among you must be your servant, and whoever would be first among you must be slave of all" (Mark 10:43–44).

If the people in charge all over the world understood this truth, what a blessing it would be for mankind! It is a pity that many civil servants do not bear the mentality of a "servant." They are too keen to dominate and determine the fates of others, to "rule over others," and even abuse their positions for personal gains, putting their own interests above those of the community.

The teaching of Jesus is powerful because He set an example first, and He was able to say, "The Son of man came not to be served but to serve, and to give his life as a ransom for many" (Matt. 20:28). He was born among us two thousand years ago and lived with us. He came from Heaven and fulfilled the prophecy of Isaiah about the "suffering servant": He bore our sins, resisted all kinds of temptations (Heb. 4:14–16), was tortured and persecuted, sacrificed His life, and became our sin offering.

In the past two thousand years, have the apostles and their successors been imitating their Master Jesus and practicing the servant spirit? Religious leaders are easily deified. The more deified they are, the greater the temptation to "rule over people." To remind themselves constantly of this truth, the popes call themselves "the servant of servants." In the traditional liturgy, whenever the pope presided over a solemn ceremony, someone would burn a small piece of flax before him and say, "Holy Father, so passes the glory of the world." *Sic transit gloria mundi!*

Modern people of God are conscious of their rights more than ever before, and it may be more effective in preventing the emergence of "bureaucracy" within the Church. There are more and more excellent examples among pastors. Pope John XXIII is generally regarded affectionately as the "the Good Pope." The last Italian bishop of Hong Kong, Lorenzo Bianchi, and the last Portuguese bishop of Macau, Arquimínio Rodrigues da Costa, were both modest and good men.

St. Augustine said, "What I am for you terrifies me; what I am with you consoles me. For you I am a bishop; but with you I am a Christian."[9] When we recall that Jesus is the role model we must follow, we cannot help but feel terrified. It is not easy to be a suffering servant and sacrifice oneself, but at the same time, remembering that Jesus is also the cornerstone we can depend upon fills us with confidence.

Jesus, being our sin offering, has prolonged life for us, His descendants. We have been redeemed by His sufferings, and we regained our right to be children of our heavenly Father (see Isa. 53:10–11). We know that He has experienced all kinds of temptations and was able to understand us. We can "with confidence draw near to the throne of grace, that we may receive mercy and find grace to help in time of need" (Heb. 4:14–16).

To preach, and to evangelize are to introduce this great priest, the only Savior, to the entire world. How the people need Him!

[9] Quoted in *Lumen Gentium* 32.

"Star" priests

What's wrong with being a "star" apostle or a "star" priest? There is nothing wrong with it.

The saints are all unwilling stars. But deliberately being a "star" apostle or a "star" priest is dangerous because the goal is wrong. What "stars" do is no longer for God but for their cause. God has no responsibility to help them succeed.

It is natural, and possibly objective, to have a good impression of a particular priest or a special appreciation for a specific preacher. But it would be dangerous if "appreciation" became "worship" because only God is worthy of our worship. It is also dangerous if the worship mentality produces a sense of possession because priests belong to the Church and the laity. No individual faithful or parish can grasp them selfishly.

In conclusion, if we put the risen Christ at the center of the Church, all will be good; if we put ourselves or individuals at the center, there will be many problems. What happened in the Church at Corinth is worth remembering.[10]

[10] See 1 Corinthians 1:10–17, in which St. Paul warns against factions in the Church.

In his post-synodal apostolic exhortation *I Will Give You Shepherds* (*Pastores Dabo Vobis*), Pope John Paul II listed several main obstacles to accepting the call to a vocation:

1. *Material wealth.* Just as the rich man mentioned in the Gospels did not have the courage to accept the call of Jesus and "went away sorrowful; for he had great possessions" (Matt. 19:22), modern youth can easily fall into the temptation of the consumer society and be controlled and imprisoned by hedonism. "There is a refusal of anything that speaks of sacrifice and a rejection of any effort to look for and to practice spiritual and religious values."[11] But there are more fundamental factors that make understanding and accepting vocations more difficult, if not impossible.
2. *Confusion about the concept of God*, viewing God as a Master who only wants us to submit to Him, or seeing vocation as a heavy burden. Many have forgotten the true face of God that Jesus revealed

[11] *I Will Give You Shepherds* 8.

to us: He is a loving and caring Father who treats us as friends and His children.

3. Modern people also have some *distorted ideas about humanity*: some think that people cannot inherently be free at all, and everything is controlled and determined by external factors, while others suggest that human freedom means a complete lack of restraints from morality or standards. Egocentrism is also widespread, and many no longer understand the value in serving their communities.

In such a cultural background, to promote vocations, we must first revive the "Christian values": believing that in Christ, by participating in His loving sacrifice, we can realize our human potentials, build a harmonious human family, and move toward happiness in eternal life.

The People of God

Living stones for the building of a spiritual temple

In the previous paragraphs, we reflected mainly on the role of the leaders in the Church. The leaders are the servants of the people. They are workers in the vineyard of the Lord. The people are the vineyard, the kingdom of God on earth. The leaders are the shepherds; their duty is to lead the sheep to the heavenly pastures.

Too commonly when "Church" is mentioned, they think about the bishop in his cathedral or even the cathedral itself. Now, the etymology of the word *Ecclesia* (Church) means "the gathering of the people."

It is true that the important thing is to worship in spirit and truth, but it is also very desirable to have beautiful church buildings where people can gather. But the most important thing is to remember that the apostles said that we are the living stones with which the spiritual temple is to be built.

The Basilica of St. John Lateran is the first basilica of the Church built by Emperor Constantine in the area of the Lateran Palace. The universal Church started to celebrate the anniversary of the dedication of the basilica in 1565 because this is the cathedral of the pope and is therefore honored as the mother church of the Church in Rome and worldwide. On that day, we first of all have to give thanks to God, for He, the infinite goodness, is willing to make His dwelling among us.

1. The book of Samuel recalls the prayer of Solomon when he dedicated the temple to the name of the Lord. He wondered and said: "Behold, heaven and the highest heaven cannot contain thee; how much less this house which I have built!" (1 Kings 8:27; 2 Chron. 6:18). But God did say, "My name shall be there" (1 Kings 8:29) and "My name may be there for ever" (2 Chron. 7:16).

How blessed are the faithful of the New Testament era! We have Jesus in the consecrated Host in our churches. Before leaving the world, He established such a wonderful way for us to continue to experience His presence. Every time the Church celebrates Mass, whether in a grand basilica or a simple chapel, the holy disciples in Heaven and on earth will gather together through the Word and the Body. After Mass, we can also adore Jesus in the Eucharist, to sing His praises and to present to Him our prayers.

The faithful cherish these blessings. Faithful generations after generations built those renowned churches that became the destinations of pilgrimages. They gave money and labor so that they could engrave the content of faith on walls and windows by using precious materials and artists' ideas.

2. Grand basilicas are only a means; they aim to "worship God in Spirit and truth." Jesus said, "we worship what we know" (John 4:22). Only when God reveals Himself to us can we worship Him. He is our Creator and Savior; we "praise Him, bless Him, adore Him, glorify Him and give Him thanks." The sacraments, instituted by Christ, and the liturgies of the Church help us live out our Faith. Baptism, which makes us die and come back to life with Christ, brings us to the community of the Church. The Eucharist unites us, and the churches become our homes.

The truth reminds us that our home should not be limited to our parish; we belong to the same diocese. A diocese is also known as a local Church. The head of the diocese is the bishop, the successor of the apostles. We read the names of the bishops during Mass, and every priest is an assistant to the bishop.

Yet our home should not be limited to our diocese. We belong to the universal Church, and the faithful all over the world are all our brothers and sisters.

The Basilica of St. John Lateran is the cathedral of the pope, but the pope now resides next to St. Peter's Basilica. The development of communication technology gives us more opportunities to experience the universality of the Church. St. Peter's Square has almost come to be the home of every one of us. In any case, the important thing is that we have a Supreme Pontiff in Rome, the successor of the Prince of the Apostles and the Vicar of Christ. He is the pillar of the truth and "the chairman of charity." The world is becoming increasingly chaotic, and the dictatorship of relativism is becoming more and more domineering. But we are blessed that popes in modern times are not afraid of criticising this dictatorship of relativism. They insist on the truth and promote charity, being the rudder for the directing of our lives, like a lamp that illuminates the path of mankind.

3. We repeat, leadership is essential and indispensable. But the Church is a community in which everyone has a part to play. It is like the construction of a basilica. After the foundation stone is laid, other pieces of stone are placed. Everyone who "worships God in Spirit and truth" is a living stone (see John 4:23; 1 Pet. 2:5). Every piece of stone should first be chiseled neatly to match the whole plan. That is to say, each of the faithful should cultivate himself and recognize his role and position in the community.

The vine and the branches

Jesus is the vine, and we are the branches. The Church is also the vine, and we are her branches as well.

Acts 9:26–31 tells the story of Paul's first visit to Jerusalem to meet Peter and the other apostles. Luke seems to want us to understand that Paul went to Jerusalem immediately after his conversion. But in chapter 1 of the Letter to the Galatians, Paul emphasized that after he was directly called by Jesus, he did not immediately go to see those the twelve apostles before him. He went to Jerusalem to see Peter only three years later and stayed with him for a mere fifteen days. Chapter 2 mentions that Paul went to Jerusalem again after fourteen years and "laid before them (but privately before those who were of repute) the gospel which I preach among the Gentiles, lest somehow I should be running or had run in vain" (Gal. 2:2). Although he had accepted the Gospel directly from Jesus Christ, he still acknowledged the need to be consistent with the other apostles, especially with Peter, the patriarch of the apostles, in order to ensure the unity of faith.

The unity of faith was not easily achieved. Luke candidly recorded the tension between Judaism and Hellenism in the early days of the Church, and how the apostles in Jerusalem would hardly have accepted Paul had it not been for the mediation of Barnabas.

The unity of faith is still not easily achieved. In this modern world full of chaotic thoughts, how can we not cherish the unity of faith in our Church? This unity of faith does not exclude reasonable and healthy diversity, but diversity should never become relativism, and contradictory principles should not be established side by side. To insist on a position that contradicts the teaching of the Church is to be intentionally divisive.

To maintain the unity of faith, while promoting the renewal and deepening of our understanding of faith, pastors and theologians in the Church have different missions and roles.

A Church in mission

I have always disliked the Chinese translation of the name *Mission Sunday* (宣傳). It seems to mean "propagating" (宣傳) our Church (教會). The word *mission* comes from the Latin *mittere* (it means "to send" in English), which also means "to dispatch." Its theological significance brings us back to the mystery of the Trinity. God is one and triune, in that the Father generates the Son, the Father loves the Son, the Son loves the Father, and the love between the Father and the Son is the Holy Spirit—eternal love and eternal joy.

God has decided from eternity to share His goodness with men so that it begins a new chapter in the history of love. The crucial event of this history is that the Father "sent" His Son, who became incarnate. The Son assumed humanity so that man might share in His divinity. The Son fulfilled His mission on earth and "sent" the Holy Spirit with the Father. Then they "sent" the apostles under the guidance of the Holy Spirit to announce the gospel of His love to the world.

The theme of Matthew 22:35–40 is "the Commandment of Love." The words of Jesus come from chapter 6 of the book of Deuteronomy, which is the prayer that the Jews recite three times a day, "Hear, O Israel: The Lord our God is one Lord; and you shall love the Lord your God with all your heart, and with all your soul, and with all your might" (vv. 4–5). The book of Deuteronomy then outlines the history of God's love for Israelites. He swore to the "father of a multitude of nations" (Gen. 17:4) and delivered the Israelites from Egypt. God first loved men, and men should keep the commandment of love.

The history of God's love unfolds in the Old Testament, and the Gospel is the final version of this history of love. What is prophesied in the Old Testament becomes a reality in the New Testament. God's love is finally manifested fully in Jesus, and God brings salvation through the blood of His Son.

John Paul II said in the encyclical *Redemptoris Missio* that the Second Vatican Council asked us to be optimistic about the universal salvation of mankind. However, it is still our duty to proclaim Jesus. A Synod of Bishops for Asia recognized that other religions also have the seed of the Word and the elements of salvation. It also emphasized, however, that we should still recognize Jesus is the only Savior of mankind and that all grace comes from Him.

The responsibility of proclamation remains the same, but we should pay more attention to our attitude and method.

First, regarding our "attitude," we must not be arrogant when announcing the gospel, as if we are better than others. We are only more blessed and have first heard the good news of the gospel. Just as St. Paul said to the Thessalonians, "you received the word in much affliction, with joy inspired by the Holy Spirit" (1 Thess. 1:6), we must not hide this joy in our hearts but run to the housetops and proclaim loudly so that everyone knows the good news. Asian bishops said our hearts would not be at ease unless this good news reached people all over Asia.

The most basic mentality of the evangelizer is gratitude—knowing that what we have received is far more than we can give. It is, of course, not difficult to have a humble attitude. With this humble attitude, proclamation becomes conversations that are equal and respectful to others.

Second, regarding our "method," there are many ways to evangelize, but the most important is through love, the only tool to convey love. The Synod of Bishops for Asia emphasized the "witness of love." Evangelization is a matter of the "heart"; precisely a matter of love. God first loved us, and we must love in return. This is the First Commandment. The Second Commandment is similar to the first one: love your neighbor as yourself (see Matt. 22:37–39). Others should see the love of Christ in us, as the Thessalonians saw it in Paul.

Exodus 22:20–26 lists some people God wants us to care about particularly: foreigners, widows, orphans, the poor . . . We can continue the list with the sick, the elderly, the disabled, the mentally disabled, disaster victims, new immigrants . . . The vulnerable are those the Church serves as a priority.

Charity has always been a characteristic of Church services. It is not a means used only for the purpose of evangelization but, by itself, is a sincere testimony of life. No doubt it also has the effect of evangelizing. Evangelization and social concern are the same charitable love manifested differently.

Some decades ago, Pope John Paul II canonized the founders of two missionary societies, Daniel Comboni of the Comboni Missionary Society and Arnold Janssen of the Divine Word Missionary Society. He also canonized Joseph Freinademetz, the Divine Word missionary who worked in China, and later canonized Mother Teresa of Calcutta, founder of the Missionaries of Charity.

Missionaries, both men and women, leave their families and countries for faraway lands. As strangers they have to learn about different cultures and adapt themselves to new life situations. They face difficulties and even hostility for no purpose other than to bring the gospel to those to whom they are sent: their new brothers and sisters. They make Jesus' desire their own; they want to quench His thirst.

The sacrifices of the missionaries laid the foundations of the Church in China and in Hong Kong. The missionaries irrigated this vineyard of God with their sweat and blood. Even today our diocese relies on their support. May God bless them and reward them.

The diocese has shown its increasing maturity through its participation in the mission *ad gentes* (to foreign countries). Our Catholic Lay Missionary Association was established in 1988 and has twenty-one members who have gone on mission to Africa and Cambodia.

When St. Joseph Freinademetz asked his bishop to allow him to follow his missionary vocation, the bishop gave this answer: "As bishop of Bressanone [Brixen], I say no, but as a bishop of the Catholic Church I say yes, go, my son, and be a good missionary." Our diocese is suffering from a dire shortage of priests, but we must still be thankful that God has made us part of the Church's missionary endeavor. He will reward us with many vocations for our diocese. When Fr. Paul Kam asked me for permission to be a missionary in Africa, I gave the same answer as the bishop of Bressanone.

The examples of our sisters and brothers who leave for the foreign missions serve to encourage us to take up our missionary role more seriously. The Church is not a private club. So when we pray and sing in our churches, we should not forget friends who are still wandering outside in the dark. Our Lord wants them to join us too. We should not have peace until they are with us.

Every time I gaze on our city from the Peak, one of the highest spots in Hong Kong, or look at the thousands of illumined windows at night, I tell the Lord, "The family You have entrusted to me is so big. How can I manage?" I believe I hear His voice replying: "Joseph, do you love me? Shepherd my sheep!" Sisters and brothers, do you hear the same voice calling your name?

A Church of martyrs

When I was teaching in a seminary in China, I prayed with priests and seminarians every day. During this period, I suddenly discovered that "sacrifice for the Faith" was mentioned in the Church's liturgy many times. There were a lot of feasts dedicated to the martyrs. The Mass readings and the psalms always mentioned the suffering of the prophets and the righteous, and Jesus and the apostles suffered persecution.

Beginning with Stephen, generations of martyrs have confirmed the prophecy of Jesus. The history of martyrdom in the Roman Church is particularly glorious.

The history of the Church mission is a history of martyrdom. Our Church in China has also written a glorious page.

Pope John Paul II specifically mentions modern martyrs in his apostolic letter *Tertio Millennio Adveniente*: "*In our own*

century the martyrs have returned, many of them nameless, "*unknown soldiers*" as it were of *God's great cause*" (no. 37). The pope encourages us to gather necessary documentation about them.

Martyrdom does not necessarily involve bloodshed, and the deeds of martyrdom do not necessarily have to be spectacular. Cardinal József Mindszenty of Hungary was arrested and imprisoned many times in those years. As he was well known in the world, they were somewhat afraid of him and released him after a few days of imprisonment. He suffered but always retained a kind of dignity—until one day, when they dragged him to a burrow, stripped him of his clothes, and began beating him. Only then did he realize that no one would treat him as anything anymore. No friends could help him anymore. This is what martyrdom looks like.

It is natural for people to cherish life. When they are in trouble, they first ask for help. Psalm 69 says, "But as for me, my prayer is to thee, O Lord. / At an acceptable time, O God, / in the abundance of thy steadfast love answer me" (v. 13). The martyrs can finally face death unflinchingly because they understand the significance of sacrificing one's life for God.

In the book of Revelation, we read the vision of John when he was caught up in spirit after being exiled to the island of Patmos (1:9–11, 12–13, 17–19). The Church was then persecuted by enemies from the outside. At the same time, it was internally endangered by heresy and indifference. The purpose of the revelation was "to strengthen those faithful whose faith was wavering and to encourage the righteous persons who suffer because of their faith" with the manifestation of the glory of Christ and the final victory.

The Church at that time had already left the room of the Last Supper and was far away from the Temple in Jerusalem. The Church today is in a similar situation: secularism, philosophical materialism, atheism ... For the faithful of today, the vision of Revelation brings much needed comfort and encouragement.

"I saw ... one like a son of man, clothed with a long robe and with a golden girdle round his breast" (Rev. 1:12–13). All the encouragement and comfort come from Jesus Christ, who appeared as the Son of Man. Chapter 7 of the book of Daniel talks about His status: "He came to the Ancient of Days.... And to him was given dominion and glory and kingdom, that all peoples, nations, and languages should serve him;

his dominion is an everlasting dominion, which shall not pass away, and his kingdom one that shall not be destroyed" (vv. 13–14). The robe signifies He is a priest (see Exod. 28:4), and the golden sash signifies He is a king (see 1 Macc. 11:58).

The message given by this Son of Man to the Church of that time is also what we need for our Church today. He said, "Fear not, I am the first and the last, and the living one; I died, and behold I am alive for evermore, and I have the keys of Death and Hades" (Rev. 1:17–18).

"Do not be afraid!" was the greeting Jesus usually said when he appeared to His disciples after His Resurrection. That was also the pet phrase of Pope John Paul II since the day he was elected. What are we afraid of? Difficulty, suffering, failure, or loneliness? What we fear most is death! Jesus tells us that He has conquered death completely; He is life, the eternal life.

The apostles were not prepared to welcome the great news of the Resurrection. But when the living Jesus stood before Thomas, Thomas cried out, "My Lord and my God!" (John 20:28).

The apostles came to believe in Jesus of Nazareth, who rose from death; and by His power they performed miracles.

There is certainly a greater miracle: these apostles, who were sinners themselves, became the tool of the Holy Spirit to forgive the sins of others.

The book of Revelation has been a "theological reflection" on the Roman Empire and has left us with a fundamental "theology of history." History is constructed by autonomous man, and God will not take away the autonomy of man. Yet, after His Resurrection, Christ becomes the Lord of history. Autonomous man would have to make a choice: to follow Him or not to follow Him.

Those who do not follow Him and stubbornly commit sins would exclude themselves from life, and those who follow Him no longer need to worry about fighting alone. He not only gave us a set of commandments but also gave us the strength to practice them. He forgives us and lifts us up to fight again when we fall.

Journeying toward the eternal life He brings, we faithful have nothing to fear. Countless frail men and women, elderly and children, from generation after generation, have not feared the threat of kings and have not surrendered to the temptation of the secular world. They insist on recognizing Christ as their only Savior and taking the Gospel as their rules of life. Let us always take part in the team of "the saved."

Love stronger than death

Cardinal Carlo Maria Martini, former archbishop of Milan, liked to preach a series of retreats once a year. He often based his preaching on one book of the Bible. I once used his meditation on the book of Jeremiah for animating a retreat and used it again later. I feel deeply touched when I read it (see Jer. 38:4–6, 8–10).

The prophet who shared sorrows more than good news was once thrown into the mud of a cistern. In the worldwide trend of libertarianism, those who hold to the Lord's Ten Commandments are judged as stubborn, outdated people, and those who accept the Church teaching are regarded as the "fanatics."

The fate of Jesus was no better than Jeremiah's. Jesus did good deeds everywhere but did not cease to be the target of the opposition. When He was born, the angels proclaimed peace, but in Luke, Jesus says that He has come to establish division (12:49–53). Of course, it is not that He is dividing us, but everyone needs to make a choice before Him. In this way, He indirectly and passively becomes the cause of division.

Some shouted "Hosanna!" and others shouted, "Crucify Him!" Those who cried out "Hosanna!" failed to help Him avoid the trap of His enemies. He finally died on the Cross, accused of "destroying traditional religion" and "being politically incorrect." The followers will not be better than their Master. "A cloud of" followers in generations have embarked on the same *via dolorosa* (see Heb. 12:1).

Love is sweet, but love can be "fiercer than death" (see Song of Sol. 8:6). Jesus uses fire and water to describe it. The power of fire and water can be very fierce, and nothing can stop their momentum. Fire can burn everything away, and water can wash everything away. Whereas benefits can be measured and compromised, love cannot. Love has to be thorough and comprehensive. It is not afraid of bloodshed and does not spare life. The love for God requires us to "place righteousness above loyalty to family." God cannot let us not love Him above all things and people. It is only by doing this that we can possess Him. Possessing Him is our true happiness. Possessing Him makes us able to love others.

Soteriological and eschatological considerations

Up to now, we have analyzed, above all, the ecclesiological aspect of the journey of the pilgrim Church toward the heavenly Jerusalem; that is, who leads the People of God on this pilgrimage and how. Let us now take an overall look at this historical reality.

For us, history is the history of salvation, it is soteriology, but this history has already entered the end times, because salvation is already objectively achieved with the first coming of the Lord Jesus. But we still await His Second Coming, when eschatology will have its perfect fulfillment.

Salvation is for everyone

The prophets themselves might have been surprised that the Gentiles could enjoy God's salvation. They could go up to God's holy mountain, enter God's temple, and share the joy of God's house! They were also qualified to offer sacrifices to God! How could it be? Was it not sacrilege for the Gentiles to go into God's temple? The universality of salvation taken for granted by us was inconceivable in the time of prophet Isaiah.

God's mysterious and unpredictable plan is generally gradual; however, men's slowness creates resistance. They hesitate at a certain stage, thinking they have reached their goal. God's plan is like concentric circles that expand one after another; however, men regard the circle as a prison that prevents the momentum of expansion. The "chosen people" are tools in God's plan of salvation; however, the tools have their own limitations. They take and keep for themselves what should be shared with others. They exclude those who should be welcomed and short-listed. When Jesus came, He made great efforts to break the deadlock.

Jesus' words in Matthew 15:21–28 sound harsh, "I was sent only to the lost sheep of the house of Israel.... It is not fair to take the children's bread and throw it to the dogs" (vv. 24, 26). It represents the general mentality of the Jews at that time, which was a so-called traditional opinion. I am afraid that the apostles quite agreed after hearing this comment and were surprised by the Catholic views in the New Testament, in which it said that the Gentiles could be saved as long as they believed in God's infinite love. For them, it seemed to be a new truth that had never been heard. This new truth that needed to be understood by the apostles and accepted by the early Church still required much sacred work. After Peter baptized Cornelius and his family, he still had to explain much to the group. Saul finally succumbed to the light and sound from Heaven and became an Apostle to the Gentiles. His mission was to evangelize the Gentiles. But he couldn't escape his Jewishness, and the Lord didn't ask him to. Salvation is for everyone—the Jewish people as well. Although the Jews appeared to have rejected salvation, Paul still loved his fellow citizens, who were also Jesus' fellow citizens. He did not despair of them. Paul preached the gospel to the Jews first wherever he went. But unfortunately, they rejected him most. The Jews' rejection seemed to create an opportunity for the gospel to be spread to the Gentiles, but Paul still hoped that the Jews would also repent and accept the gospel. And then his joy would be fuller.

Paul finally listed the complete reason for his hope in the salvation of the Jews: they were sinners too! We sinners can have the opportunity to obtain God's mercy because we are miserable. We are qualified because we need Him. Of course, we have to realize that we need Him, and we have to admit that we need Him!

Besides our humble acknowledgment of our helplessness, another reason that prevents God from refusing our prayers is our love for others. The Canaanite woman in Matthew 15:21–28 had a daughter who was suffering from being tormented by a demon. She loved her daughter, for whom she asked the great prophet Jesus for help. She firmly believed that if this prophet were the King of Heaven, He would sympathize with her and listen to her prayers. Nothing could shake her faith. Jesus threw cold water on her request and said that He did not come to care for the Gentiles like her and that the Gentiles were like dogs. He would perform miracles only for the children of God. She neither cared about being "rejected" nor minded being "insulted." She still firmly believed that God would rescue her daughter through the prophet.

We are accustomed to complaining that prayer is useless and that we cannot get what we ask, because we often ask for favors only for ourselves. Let's forget about ourselves, pay more attention to the pain and difficulties of others, and pray for them. Maybe we will see miracles happen at any time.

"My sheep . . . shall never perish. No one shall snatch them out of my hand. My Father, who has given them to me, is greater than all, and no one is able to snatch them out of the Father's hand" (John 10:27–29). How comforting it is: God the Father and the Son hold us tight, allowing no one to snatch us away!

The significance of the Resurrection of Jesus is that He has truly accomplished salvation for every one of us. He has fulfilled the purpose of the Father's creating us: He will be our God and we shall be His people.

To say that Jesus is the only Savior is to affirm the universality of salvation and to deny any exclusion or discrimination: everyone is equally important and precious in the eyes of God. God is willing to pour out His blood for everyone.

In the days of the early Church, it was difficult for the narrow-minded Jews to accept this truth. Before baptizing the family of Cornelius, Peter said, "every one who believes in him receives forgiveness of sins through his name" (Acts 10:43). But when Peter returned to Jerusalem, the circumcised believers confronted him, and he struggled to justify his actions. Finally, they understood and said, "Then to the Gentiles also God has granted repentance unto life" (Acts 11:18).

Paul and Barnabas encountered similar resistance in Antioch of Pisidia. The Gentiles were delighted when they heard the Lord had said to Paul, "I have set you to be a light for the Gentiles, that you may bring salvation to the uttermost parts of the earth" (Acts 13:47). But the Jews, full of envy, persecuted the two apostles.

No matter how difficult the process is, the ultimate victory belongs to the Lord. The book of Revelation describes the wonderful ending: "great multitude which no man could number, from every nation, from all tribes and peoples and tongues.... For the Lamb in the midst of the throne will be their shepherd, and he will guide them to springs of living water; and God will wipe away every tear from their eyes" (7:9, 17).

Our Good Shepherd leads all the sheep to the one sheepfold. We may not know how He does it, but we are sure that when He is willing to do it, He will surely have His way. We may not know the way He uses. But He has told us what we should do. Every one of us has been "made a light for the Gentiles" and is responsible for being an instrument of salvation "to the uttermost parts of the earth." In *Lumen Gentium*, the Second Vatican Council solemnly announced that all the laity are responsible for preaching the gospel.

Salvation history is gradual

In Exodus, God compared Himself to a female eagle, bearing Israel like a baby eagle upon His wings and teaching it how to fly. This comparison helps us to imagine and understand

God's love. Israel became God's "treasured possession"—His treasure. Israel was chosen to be "a kingdom of priests, a holy nation."

Just as there was, among the Israelites, a family of priests who performed the task of mediator for all the Israelites, Israel also served as a mediator for all peoples. That is to say, all mankind belongs to God, but Israel maintained a connection with God on behalf of all mankind through the Word and the liturgy.

From another angle, the Letter to the Romans points out how great God's love is for us: when we are still "sinners," "the ungodly" and "enemies of God," the Father has sent the Son (see Rom. 5:6–11). The Son uses His blood to redeem us, justifying us and letting us reconcile with our Father. The Jews think that man should be righteous by obeying the law. Paul says, however, that we have absolutely no ability to justify ourselves. If it were not for Christ's salvation, we would not be able to obey the law at all. Salvation is freely accomplished for all; we are born in salvation.

The history of salvation progresses through stages: first for the Israelites and then for all mankind; first proclaiming the coming of the Kingdom of Heaven, and then after Jesus' Ascension, giving testimony about Jesus' Resurrection and the Kingdom of Heaven.

Salvation is accomplished, but it needs someone to bring it to everyone's heart. This task Christ entrusted first to His apostles. They were sendees, loyal servants, and plenipotentiaries. The harvest of salvation is ripe, but workers for the harvest are needed.

The core of salvation is reconciliation with God so that we may become children worthy of His love again. The main effect of salvation is the forgiveness of our sins. But there are also additional and "Messianic-aged" gifts: healing the sick, raising the dead, cleansing the lepers, and casting out demons. Jesus did these things and asked the apostles to do them too.

The Gospel says that Jesus felt compassion for the crowd because they were poor and wandering like sheep without a shepherd. Many poor and homeless people in modern society are still waiting for helping hands. Though the harvest is abundant, however, the laborers are few. The harvest laborers can be of many types, but priests have an irreplaceable role in the Church.

Some time ago,[12] because of the absence of a local minor seminary, a consensus had been made in our diocese

[12] This refers to an initiative taken during the time Cardinal Zen was titular bishop of Hong Kong (2002–2009) with the goal of giving young people the possibility to

to speed up the pace of discovering and cultivating youth vocations so that young people who aspire to religious life can grow up in an environment that helps them discern vocations. We created one "vocation group" with five young people living together. They went to school during the day, prayed together at night, and shared life experiences with the vocation director. One of these five people reached the priesthood and the others affirmed that their faith made considerable progress during that time.

Jesus wants to have collaborators

Calling and sending

The prophets of the Old Testament were shepherds of faith to the Israelites. Their vocations were often conspicuous and prominent, attracting the attention of the people to gain their trust. Many prophets received their calling in visions: Samuel learned of his vocation from the voice of God; this was a rather "spiritual" example. Before then, Samuel was not familiar with the voice of God. For many

discern vocations to the priesthood in an appropriate environment.—Ed.

prophets, God's calling was unexpected and a great shock to their lives.

Then Jesus Christ came, as God sent Him here for His work of salvation. He is in charge of this work, and all who are to participate in this shall be chosen and beckoned by Him; He is "the One who calls."

In fact, one can say "calling" represents the entire mission of Jesus Christ: He came to call on lost souls to seek our heavenly Father. But amid this general calling, He also specifically called on some people to follow Him more closely and participate more directly in His mission.

The vocation to the priesthood is an immediate concern for the Church. Let us see what insights we can glimpse from the Gospel of John:

1. God chooses His disciples through personal relationships. First, John the Baptist introduced his disciples to Jesus, and subsequently the two disciples brought their brothers to Him as well. Later, Philip, who was from the same hometown as Andrew and Simon, presented his friend Nathanael to Jesus too.

The support of parents, the encouragement of the parish community, and especially the example and guidance of predecessors who have responded to their own callings are of utmost importance to the growth of vocations!

2. Those who seek with a sincere heart will surely find their calling. After heeding John the Baptist's words, his disciples followed Jesus to the place where He lived. Andrew said to Simon, "We have found the Messiah" (John 1:41).

The human heart naturally yearns for something. What it yearns for determines what kind of person someone is. To be a person of purpose, we must pursue virtuous goals. In this exceedingly utilitarian society, we need to create opportunities for young people to understand what a wonderful goal it is to be an apostle of Jesus Christ.

3. The true "summoner" is Jesus Himself, who chooses "whom he desired" (Mark 3:13). John did not record what the two disciples saw at the place where Jesus lived, but what he experienced during those few hours had left such a tremendous impact on his mind that he even remembered the exact time—about four o'clock in the afternoon (see John 1:35–42). Jesus looked at Simon (as He "looking upon him, loved him" [see Mark 10:21]) and gave him a new name: Peter.

All efforts to advance vocations are only doing the preparation work. The ultimate goal is to lead the youth finally to Jesus Christ. Creating opportunities for young people to meet Jesus Christ in silence is the main method of developing vocations.

4. Some people think that the greatest challenge of vocation is the mandatory celibacy of priests, but I've heard that it's just as difficult to look for people who heed their calling in the Orthodox and Protestant churches.

Hong Kong society is very much like the city of Corinth in St. Paul's time. The eroticized culture exaggerates the sexual needs of humans. It almost seems that people cannot live without "sex"; or that people cannot mature without intimate relationships between men and women. What St. Paul said to the Corinthians at that time must be very helpful for young people considering vocations to the priesthood. He said, "You were bought with a price," and "you are not your own." "God raised the Lord and will also raise us up by his power." We will have a spiritual, glorious body and no longer be slaves on Earth (see 1 Cor. 6:13–15, 17–20).

Christians who live married lives should respect their new identity. The human body is a medium for expressing emotions. In married life, sex is a medium to express love, not an end in itself.

The Church tells us that, as the Gospels dictate, there is another way to glorify God besides living a virtuous married life—adhering to celibacy for the Kingdom of God. When God calls people to the priesthood, He also gives them an extraordinary heart of love: to love God with all they have and to love all people selflessly and paternally.

Those who understand, heed the call! Do not doubt or hesitate!

Humble and enthusiastic acceptance

Luke gives a vivid description: a group of experienced fishermen worked very hard for a whole night but caught nothing. But listening to the words of Jesus, they immediately caught a lot of fish. This miracle made Peter see the presence of God in Jesus. He then fell on his knees before Jesus and said, "Depart from me, for I am a sinful man." But Jesus told him not to be afraid and said, "henceforth you will be catching men" (5:8, 10).

The prophet Isaiah admitted in front of the high and lofty throne of the Lord that he was a man of "unclean lips" (6:5). It was only after the Lord used an ember to remove his wickedness that he accepted the invitation from the Lord, "Here am I! Send me!" (6:5, 8).

St. Paul the Apostle claimed that he was not fit to be called an apostle. But by the grace of God, he became a chosen instrument (1 Cor. 15:9–10).

Similarly, Mary claimed that she was the handmaid of the Lord, but she answered, "Let it be to me according to your word" (Luke 1:38). The "word" was to make her the mother of the Son of God.

God may require a man to acknowledge his unworthiness before commending important missions to him. Humility seems to be the criterion for God to choose His instrument. Some say that God is afraid of haughty men who would take away His glory. This makes it sound as if God is not willing to share His glory with us. In fact, God knows that whoever wants to take away His glory will get nothing, and those who humble themselves to become His instrument are called to share His eternal glory and joy.

Humility seems to be a less popular virtue, while self-confidence and ambition are preferred. Self-confidence is surely important, and an inferiority complex is dangerous. Humility and self-confidence are not contradictory when self-confidence is reasonable and in line with the truth. We humbly acknowledge our strengths and merits and, at the same time, objectively admit our limitations. Humble people rely on God, and their self-confidence will increase a hundredfold. With God as our stronghold, what should we fear? We will not be intimidated, no matter how heavy the task entrusted by God is. We know that God has started a good work and will give it a good result. When we succeed, we will be thankful and not boast; we were obliged to do what we did, and we are "useless servants" (Luke 17:10). When we fail (ostensibly), we will not lose heart. We know it is not a real failure because we believe in the mystery of the Cross.

Ambition, as a wish to excel, is good because it is a driving force for progress. Ambition also includes competition, urging us to present our strengths before others. It then allows others to choose and use what is better to serve society.

It is a pity that competitions can sometimes be cruel. It is painful to be outcompeted, and it is not uncommon to use unscrupulous means during competitions.

In doing the work of God, we emphasize ambition, but we do not advocate unscrupulous competition. For God's plan is always God's plan, and there is no big difference whether He chooses you or me to be His instrument.

We should not seek high positions to do God's work. God will use whomever He wants. When one needs to use unscrupulous means to fight for a high position, how can he be confident that he is doing the work of God? In deciding on his own to assume a high position, how can one be sure that he is not disturbing the plan of God?

Let us admit that we are sinners, with unclean lips, and do not deserve to be Christians, priests, or bishops. But since God has chosen us to be His prophets, apostles, and fishers of men, let us accept with humble, trusting hearts the lofty mission He entrusted to us. Let us command ourselves and do the work of God with trembling hearts.

Vocation to the priesthood

God pities those who were "like sheep without a shepherd," and thus decides to "set shepherds over them who will care for them" (Matt. 9:36; Jer. 23:4).

The topic of "shepherd" is similar to the topics of "prophets" and "apostles." There are still some distinctions, however: prophets are to speak the words of God, and apostles are sent to testify for God. These two missions basically apply to all believers, but the distinction between the shepherds and the sheep cannot be neglected.

On the one hand, the Dogmatic Constitution on the Church, *Lumen Gentium*, created during the Second Vatican Council, emphasizes the common priesthood shared by believers. It also indicates, however, that the "ministerial" or hierarchical priesthood differs not only in degree but also in essence from the common priesthood. On August 13, 1997, eight Vatican offices jointly signed and promulgated the *Instruction on Certain Questions Regarding the Collaboration of the Non-Ordained Faithful in the Sacred Ministry of Priest*, which was to remind everyone not to forget the differences between the two.

Neither the "secularization" of the clergy nor the "clergyization" of the laity is good for the Church. The sacrament of Holy Orders confers divine authority on certain persons so that they may serve their people in the ministerial priesthood. Jesus Christ has left us the sacraments to support us, the believers, in our faith life, especially the sacraments of the Eucharist and Reconciliation, which nourish our life in grace. The divine right to perform these sacraments has been passed down from the apostles to bishops and priests. Of course, God has His way of dispensing His grace and is not bound by the sacraments, but in normal circumstances, these sacraments are the indispensable and primary instruments.

Faced with a serious shortage of clergy, the diocese has taken some decisive measures: merging parishes and reducing the number of Mass centers. They are without doubt agonizing decisions. Some brothers and sisters did not agree and thought that encouraging laypeople to participate more actively in Church affairs could have resolved the issues.

We understand it better than before that believers are not just a flock of sheep to be shepherded passively. Their many identities, including prophets, priests, and kings, require them to serve the Church actively, regardless of whether there is a lack of clergy or not. They are required to fill the gap, but they can never replace the clergy.

At the beginning of 1992, Pope John Paul II gave us the apostolic exhortation *I Will Give You Shepherds*. This was the outcome of the 1990 ordinary general assembly of the Synod of Bishops. The topic of that meeting was "The Formation of Priests in the Circumstances of the Present Day." Before the conclusion of each general assembly, the pope consults the participating members about the topic of the next general assembly. The previous assembly before the 1990 one was about "the lay faithful." A number of laypeople were invited as observers. During the consultations, it was these laypeople who strongly urged that the next assembly be devoted to the priesthood.

In the introduction of the apostolic exhortation, the pope said, "Lay people themselves had asked that priests commit themselves to their formation so that they, the laity, could be suitably helped to fulfill their role in the ecclesial mission which is shared by all.... The more the lay apostolate develops, the more strongly is perceived the need to have well-formed holy priests.... The more the laity's own sense of vocation is deepened, the more what is proper to the priest stands out."[13]

[13] Pope John Paul II, *I Will Give You Shepherds* 3.

Vocation to religious consecration

We need consecrated men and women who, in their daily life, bring witness to the fundamental values of the gospel. They remind the baptized how to respond with holiness to the love of God poured into their hearts by the Holy Spirit by reflecting in their conduct the sacramental consecration that is brought about by God's power in Baptism, Confirmation, and Holy Orders.

Pope St. John Paul II said: "May the Holy Spirit stir up an abundant number of vocations to special consecration, so that these, in their turn, can encourage the Christian people to adhere ever more generously to the Gospel, and so that they can help all people to understand more easily the meaning of existence as the manifestation of the beauty and holiness of God."[14]

St. Paul says:

> For the word of the cross is folly to those who are perishing, but to us who are being saved it is the power of God. . . . Jews demand signs and Greeks seek wisdom, but we preach Christ crucified, a stumbling

[14] Pope John Paul II, Message for the 38th World of Prayer for Vocations (May 6, 2001), no. 3.

> block to Jews and folly to Gentiles, but to those who are called, both Jews and Greeks, Christ the power of God and the wisdom of God. For the foolishness of God is wiser than men, and the weakness of God is stronger than men. (1 Cor. 1:18, 22–25)

The fragile baby held in his mother's hands is the strong and mighty king.

The Church has become increasingly aware of this mysterious truth throughout history. It has gradually affirmed some of the ways of life that enable people to follow the crucified Christ more closely: a life of consecration, through which God calls through the gospel some of the faithful to follow Jesus more radically. The three holy vows (chastity, poverty, and obedience) consecrate a person completely to the Lord.

The Second Vatican Council stated in the Dogmatic Constitution on the Church, *Lumen Gentium*, that these "counsels are a divine gift, which the Church received from its Lord and which it always safeguards with the help of His grace." The faithful called by God "might enjoy this particular gift in the life of the Church … and may be of some advantage to the salvific mission of the Church.… The state … though it is not the hierarchical structure of the Church, nevertheless, undeniably belongs to its life and holiness" (43, 44).

Eschatological fulfillment

The Heavenly Church

The book of Revelation says that an angel stamped 144,000 people on their foreheads with the seal of the living God. In Revelation 7:5–8, there is a detailed explanation to the meaning of 144,000. It is the 12,000 men from each of the 12 tribes of Israel, and 12 is the perfect number.

In verse 9 of chapter 7, "a great multitude, which no one could count, from every nation, race, people" does not refer to another group of people. It is still the 144,000 people, and that is the whole of mankind who are saved.

The Church, especially after the Second Vatican Council, becomes more optimistic about the salvation of mankind. We can, and we should, desire all men to be saved. The Church has canonized some saints but never pointed out who could not be saved. We can and should desire all the deceased to be accepted in Heaven, including those who know God and love God, those who know Jesus and accepted His gospel, those who, without blame on their part, have not yet arrived at an explicit knowledge of God and with

His grace strive to live a good life,[15] those who live and die in the Church after their Baptisms, and those who are not baptized and in whose hearts grace works in unseen ways,[16] especially those God purified with sufferings.

Some biblical scholars say the Beatitudes teaching is itself a simple Good News. It was really like what the prophet Isaiah said: the good tidings were brought "to the afflicted" (61:1). The Lord has come to save us. We are all sinners and cannot save ourselves, but God has gifted us with His salvation. Luke stresses that blessed are those "socially and materially poor," while Matthew emphasizes that blessed are those "poor in spirit." But, in fact, everyone is blessed, for the Son of God became man and came to redeem us.

In eternity God planned to create man, making man able to know Him, love Him, engage in a covenant with Him, and be His friends and His children. Sin destroyed this plan. But God did not rest, and He persisted. His salvation is more wonderful than His creation. Today, we celebrate the success of God's plan achieved for many people. They have survived the time of "great tribulation" and "have washed their robes and made them white in

[15] See *Lumen Gentium* 16.

[16] See *Gaudium et Spes* 22.

the blood of the Lamb" (Rev. 7:14). They now "shall be like him" and "shall see him as he is" (1 John 3:2). They appreciate His goodness forever, and He lets them share His goodness. The more we share, the more joy and gladness it increases; with Our Lady and the saints, the joy in Heaven is even greater.

In contrast to the joys of the saints, we feel more that we are still in the valley of tears and the time of "great tribulation." But the saints give us hope and encourage us. They give us hope because they and we are in the same plan of God. As long as we do not refuse, God must accomplish His salvation in us. He paid a high price for this and will not easily lose anyone. In particular, we faithful should be more hopeful because we are already consecrated to belong to God. "We are God's children now; it does not yet appear what we shall be" (1 John 3:2).

The saints have arrived at the destination. They wave to us to encourage us who are still journeying. "We have achieved it, and so will you." Among the saints are our patron saints whom we particularly respect, the founders of our religious communities, our fellow countrymen, those we know in person, and even those predecessors who traveled with us in part of our life journey. They are no strangers to us!

Purification before entering our heavenly home

It is human nature to mourn and remember our deceased relatives and friends. What situation are they in now? Many deceased are already sharing eternal happiness with God in Heaven. We commemorate them on the solemnity of All Saints. The Church encourages us to remember another group of the dead. Although they died in the grace of God, they still need to go through a process of purification.

The Church has had this belief since the early days: someone who dies in grace but is not completely ready to go to Heaven will remain in the Purgatory for purification. For someone who did not commit a mortal sin or who committed a mortal sin but was forgiven after repentance of heart (see CCC 1431), the sin he committed no longer obstructs his salvation. Yet there remains the "temporal punishment," which means he may still have to bear some consequences of sin. Although his hatred for sin is sincere, it may not be deep enough; and the harm that sin does to his will is not yet fully recovered. He has not strived sufficiently to mend the harmful consequences caused by sin.

The consequence of venial sin is temporal punishment. But if someone does not have repentance of heart or has not striven to do penance, then the need for purification after he dies remains. The ethical life of man is complicated. Of course, there are the basic choices of our will, which will decide if we obey or betray God. Still, we must be responsible for other "secondary" choices. For example, we may start a good deed out of charity. But later, selfish considerations for personal reputation and profit may unknowingly intrude on our hearts and change the nature of our good deeds. We may not have striven to avoid the bad side effects of some of our behaviors. We do not have to wait until we die to correct it. Good will, appropriate penance, enthusiastic charity, prayer, and good deeds can all offset these temporal punishments. But if we do not offset these in our lifetime, we will have to go through the purification process after we die before going to Heaven.

The soul (the ego) is conscious after leaving the body. He immediately understands his situation. On the one hand, he knows that he has been saved and longs to see the goodness of God; on the other hand, he also knows that he is not worthy to stand in front of His majesty. This consciousness makes him love God deeply, but he blames himself for not being able to meet God immediately. In this cycle of love and pain, he gets purified. The imagery of fire is used to describe this pain. In fact, this fire is the sacredness of God that purifies souls.

Is it necessary for everyone to go through Purgatory? How long do we have to be there? These are meaningless questions with no answers. What we need to know is this: life is serious. If we neglect to cleanse our souls in this life, we must bear the suffering in Purgatory after death. We do not know if our relatives and friends are already welcomed in Heaven or are still under purification. They need our assistance if they are still going through this purification period.

Yes, we can help the souls in Purgatory. The souls in Heaven, on earth, and in Purgatory remain together in Christ, and all good deeds and graces are shared generously in this big family of God. God loves the saints in Heaven. He also cares for us who are still on the life journey and has compassion for the souls in Purgatory. He is more eager to reunite with them than they are. But His righteousness cannot be understated. The saints in Heaven and we on earth pray to our Father for the souls in Purgatory and offer to God the sacrifice of Jesus and the Church for them. God will be happy to accept them and be merciful to the souls in Purgatory. On All Souls' Day, the Church encourages us to obtain indulgences for the deceased. Priests are allowed to offer three Masses.

The souls have already left their bodies. They understand things so well and will appreciate our intercession. God loves them, and their prayer is particularly pleasing to God. Remembering them often makes us remember better the teaching of the Faith. It makes us more conscious about spiritual matters, makes us progress in love, and makes us more seriously examine our lives by doing good and avoiding evil.

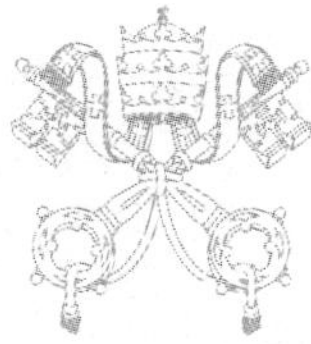

Setbacks

Unity threatened

The Lord says, "I am coming to gather all nations and tongues; they shall come and see my glory." But where shall we see the glory of the Lord? "To Jerusalem, my holy mountain," says the Lord. Is it not allowed to let the pagans enter the house of the Lord? Would it not be sacrilegious for them to enter the house of the Lord? "Some of them also I will take for priests and for Levites, says the LORD" (Isa. 66:21). All rules were overthrown, and it was a new situation unimaginable to the Israelite people.

By the time of Jesus, some Jews still resisted this significant change, fearing losing their unique status. Jesus announced the universality of the Kingdom of Heaven again: "Men will come from east and west, and from north and south, and sit at table in the kingdom of God" (Luke 13:29).

God created mankind. He loves all mankind. A chosen race is no more than an instrument with the aim of bringing salvation to all mankind.

But Jesus has come. He is the only Savior, true God and true man. Scattered because of the sin of Adam, mankind finds in Jesus the base of unity again. One Head, one Body; we are parts of the Body, and we are all one!

The Church is one, holy, catholic, and apostolic.

The *Catechism of the Catholic Church* says, "The Church is *one*" (811). This is because her source is one: the triune God. Her founder is Jesus, the only Savior; her Spirit and Advocate is the only Holy Spirit. This one Church has been marked by a great diversity, and a multiplicity of peoples and cultures is gathered together. Among the Church's members, there are different gifts, offices, conditions, and ways of life.

The Church is *catholic*. The word *catholic* means "universal," in the double sense of "according to the totality" and "in keeping with the whole."

The Church is *holy* because she receives from Christ "the fullness of the means of salvation": "correct and complete confession of faith, full sacramental life, and ordained ministry in apostolic succession" (CCC 824, 830).

The Church is *universal* because all men are called to belong to the new People of God. This people is to be spread throughout the whole world and to all ages. The Church's catholicity requires all her members to shoulder the obligation to evangelize.

Communication and information have improved, and the Church's catholicity has become more and more visible.

I had the opportunities to attend the Special Assembly of Synod of Bishops for Asia (in 1998), the plenary meetings of the Federation of Asian Bishops' Conferences, and World Youth Day in the Jubilee Year 2000. I feel proud and joyful about these opportunities. I am proud because I belong to such a great Church; I am joyful because I belong to a family united throughout the world. Rather, instead of being proud, I am honored because belonging to this Church is not of my own effort but is my blessing: through the hard work of the missionaries, I was lucky enough to know this one, catholic Church earlier than my countless countrymen. This privilege came with responsibility: many of my countrymen are waiting for me to pass this message to them.

Remembering that many of our countrymen have been barred from establishing normal ties with the Catholic Church or participating in some Catholic activities, we cannot help complaining to God, "How long will this situation continue? When will the pope be free to visit his children in China? Perhaps the words from the Letter to the Hebrews can give us some comfort, "For the Lord disciplines him whom he loves, and chastises every son whom he receives"

(12:6). Let us remain confident: after these days of suffering, we will see the abundance of "the peaceful fruit of righteousness" (Heb. 12:11).

Like those in the modern metropolis, the Church at Corinth faced many problems. We read the greetings and words of thanks in 1 Corinthians. In the opening, Paul has already implied the theme and central idea of those letters: the Church built by Christ's Body is one, holy, and catholic. This truth has shown how inappropriate the division in the Church is.

St. Paul said to the faithful in Corinth, "I appeal to you, brethren, by the name of our Lord Jesus Christ, that all of you agree and that there be no dissensions among you, but that you be united in the same mind and the same judgment" (1 Cor. 1:10). Church doctrines, Creed, and Magisterium have the effect of ensuring that the same faith can be expressed and passed on through "matching word to deed."

Sinners are constantly divided. At that time, the Corinthians were divided into groups who said that they belonged to Paul, Apollos, Peter, and Christ, respectively. It divided Christ, who had been crucified on the Cross.

Paul was reluctant to participate in this divisive operation or to allow himself to be an excuse for the division. He was by no means happy that someone had praised him. When someone denied his apostolic status, Paul vigorously defended his mission. But he knew that this mission was an errand. The primary purpose of doing so was to be loyal to the Sender, to do what he was supposed to do and recognize himself only as a useless servant, never stealing the place of the Master by placing himself in the center.

Divided loyalty

Church and state, religion and "the world"

"Render therefore to Caesar the things that are Caesar's, and to God the things that are God's" (Matt. 22:21). This famous verse is often used to prove that Jesus had affirmed the principle of "separation of Church and state." Of course, "separation of Church and state" is the consensus of the Church today, but this principle may not have such a direct relationship with this verse of the Gospel.

Pointing at the portrait and the inscription on the tax coin, Jesus replied to His enemies who tried to tempt Him:

"Render ... to Caesar the things that are Caesar's." This simply shows the excellent wisdom of Jesus, in evading their trap: they could accuse Him neither of rebellion nor of betraying the country. This statement does not mean He affirmed that the taxes of Caesar were fair.

In the context of this Gospel, Jesus saying "Render ... to Caesar the things that are Caesar's" is not a proclamation of a major principle but a tactful reply. "Render to God the things that are God's" is the great principle stated by Jesus on His own initiative without being asked by others. He said this because the Pharisees forgot about God and colluded with the pro-Roman Herodists to test Jesus. (This reminds me of Luke 23:12, which states that, at the time of Jesus' suffering, Herod and Pilate, who were enemies of each other, became friends. It also reminds me that in modern society, believers of certain opposing "ideologies" will form "unholy covenants" for the common interest.)

Jesus was not interested in politics. His mission was not to initiate a sociopolitical revolution and drive the Romans out. Trying to frame Him, the Pharisees forced him to say these words that seemed to support Caesar—"Render ... to Caesar the things that are Caesar's"—(forcing Him to be a traitor?), an act that is extremely ugly and wretched.

Jesus' mission is to lead mankind back on the path of conversion to God. What is printed on the human heart is the image and holy name of God! Jesus came to bear witness to this truth. When safeguarding the rights of the Father without compromise, Jesus put His life and death aside. In front of Pilate, He categorically admitted that He was King (completely politically incorrect!).

The mission of the Church is religious and regards the relationship between man and God. Our specialty is pastoral care and evangelization. Proclaim the great news to everyone: God is our Father, and Heaven is our home. You shall love the Lord, your God, with all your heart, with all your soul, and with all your mind. You shall love your neighbor as yourself, regardless of status, race, religion, or friendship. Every human being is an image of God.

The faithful are not only citizens of Heaven but are also citizens of this world. How do we reconcile these two identities?

The Second Vatican Council says in the Pastoral Constitution on the Church in the Modern World: "They are mistaken who, knowing that we have here no abiding city but seek one which is to come, think that they may therefore shirk their earthly responsibilities. For they are forgetting that by the faith itself, they are more obliged than ever to measure up to these duties, each according to his proper vocation."[17]

Faith also requires us to take up the mission of this world, and everyone has to fulfill it according to his own status: government officials, ordinary people, laypeople, priests, and bishops, everyone should be responsible for his own part. Sometimes you have to obey; sometimes you have to criticize. Criticism is harder than obedience. Life may not be easy for those who speak honestly and according to their consciences.

Some time ago, I read in the breviary a passage from Pope St. Gregory's *Book of Pastoral Rule*. I seriously meditated on it, and now introduce it to all you brothers and sisters: he said that being a spiritual leader of people means to decide carefully when to be silent and always to speak beneficial words. Heeding this way, the spiritual leader avoids saying things he shouldn't say or keeping silent when he should speak. As careless speech could lead to error, unwise silence could keep in a state of error a person who should be taught. Furthermore, there are some unwise pastors who worry only about losing

[17] Second Vatican Council, Pastoral Constitution on the Church in the Modern World *Gaudium et Spes* (December 7, 1965), no. 43.

the favor of others and are afraid to say what they should say publicly. According to the truth, these leaders are not like shepherds who are earnest in tending their flocks but are like hired laborers because they hide behind scenes, as shepherds run away from their flocks when wolves come.

Therefore, the Lord rebukes them through the prophet, saying, "They are all dumb dogs, they cannot bark" (Isa. 56:10). Then the Lord complained, "You have not gone up into the breaches, or built up a wall for the house of Israel, that it might stand in battle in the day of the Lord" (Ezek. 13:5). Going "into the breach" to fight against the enemy refers to defending the flock, speaking out boldly, and striking back against the power of the world. Standing "in battle in the day of the Lord" refers to resisting the forces of evil through the love of justice.

If the shepherd is afraid to say something serious, isn't such silence just like turning his back and running away? If he stands up and defends the flock, he will build a wall around the house of Israel against the attack of the enemy.

Unholy Church?

We've talked a lot about the Church's being one, catholic, and apostolic, but we talked little about her holiness. We all know very well that the Church is holy because she has all the elements to sanctify herself and also because there are many believers of every category who have lived as splendid models of holiness, which consists in a high degree of love for God and for one's brothers. But unfortunately there is also the flip side of the coin.

Let's talk about the mistakes made by men of the Church. Even today, the case of Galileo is often mentioned as proof of the obscurantist nature of the Church, but we forget that many of the most famous scientists are believers and many universities were founded by the Church. Galileo himself always remained a believer, and while he accepted the unfair condemnation of the Roman Curia, he maintained the integrity of his conscience with that "and yet it moves."

In China even today, people often bring up the "the rites' controversy" (the controversy about acts of veneration for the ancestors), which prevented the acceptance of the Catholic Faith by the emperor, who was well disposed towards it. It was a misunderstanding; those rites were not acts of worship, but, objectively for many Chinese, the survival of their ancestors ended up being the only element of transcendence in which they believed they could find a religious experience.

What about those scandals: that dispute between three pretenders who all declared themselves to be legitimate popes?

And when the infamous Borgia family managed to bring the corrupt Alexander VI to the papal throne? And the cruelties committed during the time of the Crusades? These are all things that have become possible because secular powers have managed to seize religious power.

The most damaging thing is certainly the sexual abuse scandal and the subsequent cover-ups. Rather belatedly, the Church has shaken herself, recognizing the enormous gravity of the crimes, deciding to compensate the damages, taking every measure to ensure that such crimes never happen again.

Unfortunately, some in the Church return almost complacently to these scandals, blaming it on so-called clericalism to support their proposition that the structures in the Church need complete change. The tragic reality is that the incredible success of the "sexual revolution" was able to penetrate into our Church and even infiltrate seminaries, dismantling all the traditional discipline, which is essential for the effective training of young men to become priests and for defending the clergy from worldliness.

A synodal Church

How will the Synod continue and end?

Looking at how the first session of the Synod on synodality ended, we cannot help but be amazed, because they tell us that it is not yet clear what synodality is. The cardinal relator of the Synod tells us that "we are still learning, synodality is not a concept; it is a process and it seems to be progressing well." But if there is no clear concept of synodality, with what criterion is it stated that the process was synodal and that the Church is becoming synodal?

Starting from the etymology of the Greek word—"walking together"—synodality was given as the theme of this Sixteenth Ordinary Assembly of the Synod of Bishops; a subtheme was also given: "Participation and communion for the mission."

Since it is not possible in many languages (including Chinese) to translate the word *synodality* directly, it is assumed that the subtheme is a faithful explication of the theme. So, without directly studying synodality, we began to study "how to dialogue together to walk together on the path of evangelization."

A new constitutive element?

There is a doubt to be resolved. They tell us that synodality is a fundamental constitutive element of the life of the Church, but at the same time they emphasize that synodality is what the Lord expects of us today. Participation and communion are obviously permanent characteristics of the one, holy, catholic, and apostolic Church. But doesn't saying that synodality is "the thing that the Lord expects of us today" mean that it is something new? In order not to see a contradiction in it, we must understand this invitation to synodality not as having to do something completely new but as giving a new impulse to something that has always existed in the Church.

With this understanding, our diocese has actively undertaken this *first phase of the Synod, the local one* (not belonging to any episcopal conference, due to the political situation, we have only the diocesan level of this phase and not that of the episcopal conference).

The diocese conducted 13 consultation assemblies with approximately 1,200 participants; 170 small-group "spiritual conversations" were conducted, with 930 participants. There was then an online questionnaire, and in six months 1,278 responses were collected from 150 communities; the participants must have exceeded 2,000. Through scientific methods, a synthesis of all this work shows that the most important thing for the diocese is to promote *the training* of priests and the faithful, especially young people. The themes of this training include: *parrhesia* (frankness) in expressing oneself and attention in listening; responsible participation in discernment and decisions by the established authorities; and dialogue in the Church, with society and between religions.

I was saying that the diocese did a very good job in the first preparatory phase of the Synod, but it did not study the exact meaning of the word *synodality*. By focusing the study on the generic sense of "walking together," no reference was made to the word *synod*, yet synods are a historical reality. The adjective *synodal* and the abstract noun *synodality* come from the word *synod*.

Walk together? Yes, but *in the Church* who walks together with whom? What is the goal of this journey? Is there a guide that ensures the right direction?

Precisely to answer these questions, the Dicastery for the Doctrine of the Faith commissioned its International

Theological Commission to draw up a document entitled *Synodality in the Life and Mission of the Church*. The commission worked between 2014 and 2017; the text was approved by the prefect of the dicastery and published on May 2, 2018, with the approval of Pope Francis.

This document is obviously listed among the documents that concern the theme of this Synod. But, strangely, the Synod secretariat makes little reference to it.

Reading the aforementioned document and the voluminous first introductory document of the secretariat of the Synod, I cannot dispel the perception that we are faced with two opposing visions of ecclesiology. On the one hand, the Church is presented as founded by Jesus on the apostles and their successors, with a hierarchy of ordained ministers who guide the faithful on their journey toward the heavenly Jerusalem. On the other hand, there is talk of an undefined synodality, a "democracy of the baptized." (Which baptized people? Do they at least go to church regularly? Do they draw faith from the Bible and strength from the sacraments?)

This other vision, if legitimized, can change everything —the doctrine of faith and the discipline of moral life.

Someone will cry: "Conspiracy theory!"

A hidden agenda?

They say there is no agenda, but this insults our intelligence. How can we forget that note in *Amoris Laetitia* after the two synods on the family? And that resolution on the "*viri probati*," even if it was not included in the post-synodal exhortation of the Amazon Synod?

How can we not worry when we look at the "synodal path" in Germany? A group of lay faithful, self-proclaimed representatives of the Catholic people, together with a majority, but less than two-thirds of the bishops, almost smugly mention "sex abuses," blaming them on clericalism; from there, they conclude that there is a serious problem in the structure of the Church that will require her complete overhaul (overturning the pyramid?) and that the sexual ethics of the Church must be updated to the modern culture. This synodal path has not yet been decisively repudiated. Let's remember also the movement that exploded in Holland in the aftermath of Vatican II (with the new Dutch *Catechism*) which led the Church of that country to languish today as if moribund?

It does not seem out of place to mention the case of the Anglican community. The poor archbishop of Canterbury has received a warning from the archbishops of the Global

Anglican Future Conference (GAFCON, which includes 85 percent of the world Anglican community), to repent of having legitimized homosexual unions; otherwise they will no longer recognize his position as an authority.

In the voluminous document of the Secretariat, perhaps not everyone has noticed that terrible but gratuitous statement that the most feared obstacle to synodality is *clericalism*. Clericalism is often tendentiously considered as the main cause of sexual abuse, while it is obvious that the sexual revolution has also entered in the Church and even seminaries.

And that long list of problems that only synodality would be able to help us address: Is it there simply as an inventory? Reading it, I mischievously suspected that what the drafters of the document were interested in was what was mentioned at the bottom of the list—that is, minorities with particular sexual tendencies who would be discriminated against, despised, and cruelly marginalized by the Church. (Thus, the acronym LGBTQ entered for the first time, solemnly, into a Church document!)

Concluding what has been said so far about the first preparatory phase of the Synod, I think that for the promoters of the Synod, this first phase was a great failure. From this phase, apparently, they wanted to gather an abundance of experiential facts as a foundation for all subsequent construction of the edifice of synodality.

But, first of all, many, as well as our people in Hong Kong, did not even understand what the promoters wanted. Moreover, the quantitative participation of the faithful was also discouraging. Reliable statistics say that it barely reached 1 percent, which is understandable, if we think of the insufficient time given for the consultation and of the difficulties created by Covid-19. Promoters tried to put a good face on bad luck, saying that there had been an enthusiastic response from all sides.

The continental phase

The second phase was the continental one. Finally, promoters had greater ability to direct the operation. The secretary-general and the cardinal relator, together with some "facilitators," went in person to six of the seven continental meetings to lead the consultation.

For Asia, the FABC (Federation of Asian Bishops' Conferences, which includes the Dioceses of Hong Kong and Macau, which do not belong to any episcopal conference) was obviously representative. The people summoned were those who had animated the work of the first phase and who were now well guided toward particular themes of dialogue and with a particular method.

The emphasis was still on sharing experiences, listening to the experiences of people who have no voice in the Church (the absent, symbolized by an empty chair at the table around which, in small groups, painful experiences of people excluded from the community are told). These experiences obviously aroused emotions, feelings of compassion. These were especially experiences of minorities with particular sexual tendencies and with situations of irregular "marriages," for which they are not accepted—that is—are excluded, while the Church should welcome everyone: *todos! todos! todos!* (all! all! all!)

The peculiar method used was the so-called conversation in the Spirit. In this method, we pray, and then everyone shares their experiences, and everyone listens. We pray again and talk again, this time integrating what everyone has heard. Then we pray again and check points of convergence and points of divergence. Conversation, not discussion!

But without adequate debate, how will the problems be resolved? There are problems, so we need to debate. Obviously the discussion must be based on the Word of God and the Sacred Tradition of the Church. The Holy Spirit will guide the discussion to consensus conclusions, as in the Second Vatican Council. The prayers must have been accumulated already before the meetings; in the meetings, the Spirit is there to guide everyone in the discussion.

Fr. Tony Lusvardi, a Canadian Jesuit and professor at the Gregorian University, says that the method of "conversation in the Spirit" does not come from St. Ignatius but from the Canadian Jesuits. This method is used not for discernment but to pacify the spirits before discernment, so that we do not immediately start arguing with excited souls instead of opening ourselves to the inspirations of Heaven. Moreover, he says, one cannot discern things that are already certain (if an action is already evidently sinful, one cannot discern whether one can commit it or not). Among the Jesuits, after all, the superiors command and the subjects obey *perinde ac cadaver* (like a corpse).

Imposing this method on the Synod proceedings was a manipulation aimed at avoiding discussions. It was all psychology and sociology, no faith and no theology.

Since several things mentioned were controversial, the beginning of discussion was still able to emerge in the little time left for dialogue in the assembly, with a few minutes given to anyone who wanted to speak.

The final report on this phase of participation made by the FABC, rather than responding to the issues that interested the facilitators, draws heavily on the results of the recent General FABC Conference on the occasion of the fifieth anniversary of their foundation. This General Conference was a true general mobilization. It carefully reflected on the needs present in the Church in Asia. The time coincided exactly with the beginning of the Synod process.

It seems that even this second, continental phase, still preparatory to the Synod itself, must not have satisfied the promoters of the Synod. But from the synthesis they made of it, in the *Instrumentum Laboris* for the actual Synod, we at least finally have the clear perception that the problems posed for discernment are the structures of the Church and the problems of sexual ethics.

The global phase

The third, global, phase, with those two big problems facing it, was supposed to be the real Synod that had to provide the solution to these problems. I hoped that they would return to the procedure tested by many past synods—that is, to start with the assemblies, where everyone hears everyone and the *status quaestionis* can emerge clearly; then to proceed to the laborious discussion (but without the help of the facilitators); then to conclude with the linguistic *circuli minores*, where concise deliberations are thrashed out to be offered to the Holy Father, in a confidential manner, as advice from his brothers in the episcopate.

It was my great disappointment when I saw that this phase had begun with the same method as the continental one, a method that does not favor the solution of problems. Foreseeing this eventuality, I had, as you know, attempted to incite some Synod fathers (cardinals and bishops) to insist on the procedure, but in vain; they are gentlemen and reluctant to make any gesture of opposition.

There was also a very severe warning regarding secrecy (almost pontifical) in order to avoid, they say, a lot of media chatter. There was, yes, a daily meeting with journalists, but only the "good guys," chosen by the facilitators, spoke to the journalists. To avoid media chatter, the faithful were kept in the dark about a Synod that was intended to be a model of synodality.

Among the members of the Synod with the right to vote, in addition to the bishops elected as representatives of the episcopal conferences, there were also a large number of bishops appointed by the pope, evidently with the aim of "balancing the two sides"; then there were religious men and women, while in the original system there were also the elected representatives of major superiors of clerical male congregations, who, similar to bishops, have a considerable number of ordained ministers under their jurisdiction.

But there is something more serious: *a large number of laypeople, men and women, participate in the Synod with the right to vote* (previously there had also been religious and laypeople, but as experts and observers, without the right to vote); this means that this is no longer a Synod of Bishops (just as a bottle of wine to which a lot of water has been added is no longer what it should be).

Someone said that we had forgotten synodality, while the Asians had always maintained it. But this is a big misconception. About this, His Excellency Msgr. Manuel Nin Güell, O.S.B., apostolic exarch for the Catholics of the Byzantine rite in Greece, says that, for Asians, the Synod is always exclusively of the bishops; the word *synod* is used to mean not the walking together of all the People of God but the walking together of the bishops with Our Lord Jesus Christ (we must remember that the patriarchs in the Eastern churches are not the equivalent of our Roman Pontiff, since, for every important decision, they must have the consent of the Synod of Bishops).

The pope can convene any kind of assembly to give him the advice he wants. But in synods of bishops, only bishops vote. Calling the recent hybrid assembly the first session of the Synod of Bishops involves a serious misnomer.

A matter of serious concern is the fact that in the Pontifical Yearbook (*Annuario Pontificio*), the Secretariat of the Synod of Bishops is renamed the Secretariat of the Synod. Which Synod? An Ecumenical Council is also a Synod. There is also a Diocesan Synod. From now on, will there also be this hybrid consultation assembly with the name of Synod? Meanwhile, *the true Synod of Bishops has been eliminated*—the one established by Pope Paul VI at the conclusion of Vatican II as an instrument of collegiality, that is, as a body through which the pope receives advice from his brother bishops in the episcopate!

At the end of this session, there were no deliberations. A second session had already been scheduled. So the first session must not be understood as a proper Synod but only as a further preparation for the second session, which alone can properly be called the Synod of Bishops, which will conclude with resolutions voted only by the bishops.

The laypeople already present at the "first session" may also be welcome at this true Synod, but as observers and experts, and will not vote together with the bishops. They will also be able to make interventions in the discussion, but at the invitation of the presidency, perhaps upon prior request; it is obvious that the president delegates must all be bishops.

What I have pointed out so far can be considered a problem of mere confusion of terms, but it is a dangerous confusion. It is important to call everything with its proper name, and this will also clarify the task during this year of intermission for all of us in the Church.

The Synod of October 2024

We can and must all take an interest in the coming Synod, that is, the Synod of October 2024, by organizing study sessions on the problems that the previous phases have brought to the table; study that must be done with the help of everyone (priests, men and women religious, competent laypeople), indeed, with the assiduous presence of the bishop; study accompanied by a supplement of experiences of concrete facts, so that our bishops can bring to the Synod the smell of their sheep (only they are able to bring to the Synod the true situation of their Church, the pope cannot get the smell of all his sheep in the world, especially if these are in the periphery).

But above all, in this year, there is a need for a study that will help true discussion at the level of faith; knowledge of the Constitution on the Church (*Lumen Gentium*) of Vatican II and of the aforementioned document on synodality of the International Theological Commission will be of utmost importance.

There is also a document from the International Theological Commission (Sensus Fidei *in the Life of the Church*, 2014), which explains the true meaning of the *sensus fidelium*.

Fiducia Supplicans

Before Christmas, December 18, 2023, came the declaration *Fiducia Supplicans* from the Dicastery for the Doctrine of the Faith, which justifies the blessing of homosexual couples in certain circumstances. The signatory is the prefect of the Dicastery, with the signed consent of the Holy Father. The document was at first a surprise, and then a great confusion followed. A press release of January 4, 2024, looked like half a retraction of the previous declaration.

Surprise, first of all. Before the start of the Synod, we five cardinals had asked Pope Francis five questions or *Dubia*, to which we hoped to have a clear answer, thus saving discussion time at the Synod. Within twenty-four hours, with incredible speed, a long answer came. The author could not have been the Holy Father himself but had to have come from the arsenal of the Secretariat of the Synod, prepared to counter contrary opinions. The declaration *Fiducia*

Supplicans, On the Pastoral Meaning of Blessings, merely developed that already long response to the *Dubia*.

A most unpleasant surprise. Since the problem had already come to the table, it was more than reasonable to wait for the next session of the Synod, after serious discussion, to provide a solution. Preempting such a discussion is an act of incredible arrogance and disrespect for the Synod fathers.

Despite the repeated protestation in the declaration that confusion must be absolutely avoided in such matters, the declaration has inevitably caused great confusion and threatens a serious division never before seen in the Church.

Addenda dated February 22, 2024

The establishment of ten study groups has been announced, and to them the pope has entrusted the task of a theological and juridical study on problems that emerged from the first session of the Synod of Bishops. The groups will have to deliver the results of their studies to the Holy Father in 2025. It seems that these groups will also have to inform the bishops of the Synod about their studies. So my question is: During this second session of the Synod of Bishops, won't the bishops be able to discuss and decide on those problems? Or will the Synod have a third session? In the first session of the Synod, with the method of conversation in the Spirit in small groups (not linguistic *circuli minores*, as in tradition) there was a long process of sharing emotional experiences with very little time allowed for a theological discussion between the bishops in the assembly. Won't this possibility also exist in the next session? Then it no longer makes sense to call this a Synod of Bishops. The pope has every right to consult anyone and in any way, but it is not right to call this a Synod of Bishops. So the Sixteenth Ordinary Assembly of the Synod of Bishops must not appear in the chronology of the synods! Am I supposed to think that the Holy Father appreciates the advice of his friends more than that of his brother bishops?

About the Author

Cardinal Joseph Zen, a native of China, served as the sixth bishop of Hong Kong. He was created cardinal in 2006 by Pope Benedict XVI with the intention of working for the Church in China.

Sophia Institute

Sophia Institute is a nonprofit institution that seeks to nurture the spiritual, moral, and cultural life of souls and to spread the gospel of Christ in conformity with the authentic teachings of the Roman Catholic Church.

Sophia Institute Press fulfills this mission by offering translations, reprints, and new publications that afford readers a rich source of the enduring wisdom of mankind.

Sophia Institute also operates the popular online resource CatholicExchange.com. *Catholic Exchange* provides world news from a Catholic perspective as well as daily devotionals and articles that will help readers to grow in holiness and live a life consistent with the teachings of the Church.

In 2013, Sophia Institute launched Sophia Teachers to renew and rebuild Catholic culture through service to Catholic education. With the goal of nurturing the spiritual, moral, and cultural life of souls, and an abiding respect for the role and work of teachers, we strive to provide materials and programs that are at once enlightening to the mind and ennobling to the heart; faithful and complete, as well as useful and practical.

Sophia Institute gratefully recognizes the Solidarity Association for preserving and encouraging the growth of our apostolate over the course of many years. Without their generous and timely support, this book would not be in your hands.

www.SophiaInstitute.com
www.CatholicExchange.com
www.SophiaTeachers.org